P9-AQK-856

THEN
ONE DAY ...

"Chris Andrews might be the best pure bookmaker in Las Vegas history. He's certainly the best in our family. And that's saying a lot!"
— Art Manteris, Vice President Race and Sports Operations, Station Casinos

"Chris and I have known each other for over 50 years. We grew up together, grew in this business together, and were part of the sports betting renaissance in Nevada. I'm proud to call him a friend and colleague."
— Jimmy Vaccaro, Sports Book Executive

"A hilarious journey through the history of Nevada sports betting. Chris Andrews booked it all, bet it all, and better yet, he lived it all."
— Roxy Roxborough, iconic Las Vegas oddsmaker

"You'll find yourself immersed in these stories as you enjoy this accurate and memorable journey through some history of our great industry. Come along with Chris Andrews, one of our most respected industry members, as he takes you along in *Then One Day* …."
— Vinny Magliulo, Gaughan Gaming Sports Director

"A person who can hold people spellbound when they talk is said to be a great storyteller. A person who can make others laugh, I mean really belly laugh, is said to be a great comic. What do you call someone who can do both at the same time, then whisper a meaningful secret in your ear about family, friends, relationships, and even the absurdity of life? Read on and let me know if you come up with a term for it."
— Zach Franzi, cousin, legal bookmaker, professional sports bettor

"Chris Andrews has been on a life journey that many dream of, but few can speak of with knowledge. *Then One Day* … is an enthralling read. Chris allows us to share in his incredible life ride—the highs, the unexpected, the sometime disappointments framed in the honesty of Chris and his unique way of many times seeing the humor in some of life's circumstances … as only a true bookmaker can."
— Sonny Vaccaro, sports-marketing innovator, athlete advocate

"*Then One Day* … is right on point as to how our treasured business of bookmaking worked in the past and it should be the paradigm going forward. Chris Andrews doesn't hold back in telling how it was! This book is better than a comeback of 21 points in a football game to cover the spread!"
— Vic Salerno, USBookmaking

THEN
ONE DAY ...

40 YEARS OF
BOOKMAKING IN NEVADA

CHRIS ANDREWS

HUNTINGTON PRESS • LAS VEGAS, NEVADA

Then One Day ...
40 Years of Bookmaking in Nevada

Published by: Huntington Press
3665 Procyon Street
Las Vegas, Nevada 89103
Phone (702) 252-0655
e-mail: books@huntingtonpress.com

Copyright ©2019, Chris Andrews
ISBN: 978-1-944877-19-4

Cover photos: Typewriter ©Eyewave | Dreamstime.com
Production & design: Laurie Cabot

All rights reserved. No part of this publication may be translated, reproduced, or transmitted in any form or by any means, electronic or mechanical, including photocopying and recording, or by any information storage and retrieval system, without the express written permission of the copyright owner.

Dedication

To Uncle Jack, the most respected and wisest man I have ever known, who brought me into and taught me about a life envied by so many.

Acknowledgments

Thanks to:

Michal Gaughan for giving me my first real decision-making job and recommending me for the Cal Neva position that changed my life even though I was only 25 years old, for hiring me for what I hope is my last job, and for being a friend even when I wasn't working for you.

Frank Toti for your support and sage advice. And though it would surprise people who don't know you well, for being one of the kindest and most generous people I've ever met.

Jimmy Vaccaro for being my *consigliere* every day at the South Point and throughout my life.

Roxy Roxborough for teaching me so much about this business and helping at every step of my career.

Vic Salerno for being such a worthy competitor and yet such a loyal friend. I can never repay you for helping me through some of my darkest days.

Gill Alexander, a special thanks for giving me the platform to tell these stories in the first place. Without you, this book would not be possible.

Vinny Magliulo for recommending me for the VSiN team, helping with my handicapping, and being a friend for nearly 40 years.

Brian and **Todd Musburger** for creating VSiN and making me a part of such a wonderful project.

Brent Musburger for your professionalism in guiding the VSiN team and treating me so well despite being on broadcasting's Mount Rushmore.

Ryan Growney for the ability to have such an attention to detail and yet not be a micromanager, as well as supporting me through some wild swings—sports books win and lose some awfully big decisions.

Warren Nelson for being my strongest supporter in my early years at Cal Neva.

Leon and **Steven Nightingale** for your support as my career progressed at Cal Neva.

Bill Thornton for your friendship and encouragement at Cal Neva and Against the Number.

Bill McHugh and **Jeff Siri,** my two CEOs at Cal Neva, who stuck with me through the highs and lows all bookmakers experience.

John, Michonne, and **Stephen Ascuaga, John Farahi, Bill Paganetti,** and the **Carano family** for allowing me and the Cal Neva to put our sports books in your properties. As the top operators in Reno, you folks gave us the credibility we needed to become successful.

Barry Philips, a real radio pro, for having the courage to put me on your show despite my having absolutely zero experience in that field.

John Falenski for your handicapping ability that you were kind enough to share with me as we grew in this business together.

Nick Bogdanovich for being one of the sharpest and boldest bookmakers in the world, besides being such a great friend.

Richie Baccieleri, my occasional roomie, for your handicapping ability and helping me with mine.

Jeff Whitelaw for being one of sharpest minds in our business and for having the kindness to share so much with me.

Matt Clark for establishing Against the Number with me and showing me how the power of a good handicapping platform can break down numbers to help produce winners.

Courtney Wells Fusco for helping with an early edit of this book.

James Bunting for your help in bringing this book to publication.

Anthony Curtis for making this book a reality.

Deke Castleman for your editing wisdom in putting my scattered stories in a logical order and making this book so much more readable.

Bob Martin for having the patience to teach a teenager about the bookmaking business.

Bobby Berent for explaining some handicapping secrets to a young know-nothing.

Sonny Vaccaro for making me a Roundball Classic ball boy and more and letting me see the inside of how big-time basketball works. And all the free shoes.

Jackie Gaughan for giving me a nightly masters course in the casino business by just casually chatting with me as I worked for Michael at the Barbary Coast.

My Cal Neva crew for helping me make our sports book into one of the biggest names in Nevada.

My South Point crew for being the top outfit in town and making our sports book the best in Las Vegas, and for keeping me young by being such a great group.

Art Manteris for bringing honor and prestige to our family as one of the most respected men in the sports book business.

Zach Franzi for being more than a brother since our infancy and joining me in our family's journey through this business and life.

My wife Pam for sticking with me through some of the worst times of my life. I would have never made it without you. Now that we're on a good path, I hope we can share long healthy lives for many years into the future.

Contents

Foreword
by Gill Alexander

I'm pretty sure it was the one about the rich brothers with oil money who always bet on the Twins. Or maybe the one about the old Jewish guy who used to be a boxer and routinely carried around six figures worth of cash in a bag on a bus. Or the one about the unsuspecting security guard who said he always liked Mr. Rosenthal. Y' know, because he gave him $100 just to start his car every morning.

No. It was the one about those two Twins bettors. That's what started all of this.

A bookmaker in Nevada for over 30 years, Chris Andrews and I had become friends, bonding over immigrant parents, sports history and sports betting, and good food. And then one day ... at lunch in Las Vegas sometime in 2013, he told me that first story and I immediately began thinking how I could selfishly co-opt it for my own sports betting podcast, along with the treasure trove of memories that must've surely existed in the mind from where that one had come. What was initially conceived as a sporadic five- to ten-minute tag at the end of future podcast episodes became its own weekly segment during the NFL season, affectionately entitled "StoryTime." And by that I mean to say that not a single person continued to care about anything else we discussed from that point on.

And who could blame them? There is no group in life quite as strikingly unique as sports bettors with their associated cocktail of arrogance, bravado, pop psychology, superstition, confirmation bias, and bluster. (I could go on, but I have a word limit.) At least that applies to the vast majority of them. It's why I chose to do a podcast on the subject. The mindset of sports bettors is endlessly fascinating and the real-life characters involved beat anything one could make up using one's imagination.

And that is why it's curious to me that the mainstream media that cover the sports betting industry rarely seem to lean on those who know the most on the subject, those who have been there the longest, in the heart of the matter, from the ground floor. Those who knew all the colorful personalities when shops were less corporate. Those who built Las Vegas sports betting. Those who know more through their sheer experience than the rest of us combined pretend to know. Before they're gone.

Chris Andrews not only fits that bill, having been eyewitness to or intimately involved in the array of priceless and hilarious stories you're about to read, but also remains great friends with the rest of Nevada's legendary bookmaking Mount Rushmore, so that in the event that his memory of the details has been compromised with time, we're still covered. And what was previously confined to freeform audio gets the treatment it really deserves, a full fleshing out that print affords. That, and additional stories that have previously been untold in any medium.

Enjoy these true stories from one of the truly good guys in our industry. The ensuing comedy will be trumped only by the indelible impression left on you about the human condition.

Prologue

Every little kid grows up thinking his life is normal.

I once read about parents who locked a boy in a box every night when he went to bed. He never complained, never said a word to his friends or teachers or authorities. When he was in fourth grade, he found out that's not what happens to your average kid. When he finally spoke up, people asked him why he didn't say anything sooner. He said he just thought all little boys got locked in a box at night. How would he know any differently?

It took me awhile to figure out my upbringing was different than the normal American experience. No, I wasn't locked in a box. I wasn't abused any more than any other kid who had his mother yelling at him every time he left his socks on the floor. Hell, I don't even remember ever getting spanked. Nonetheless, because of the world I grew up in, I was destined to be in the gambling business.

Don't worry. I'm no Hyman Roth lamenting to Michael Corleone, "This is the life we have chosen." Nothing nearly that dramatic and probably a lot funnier. I didn't have to make my bones or do anything more felonious than place a bet where it wasn't quite legal to do so. That world has given me a great life, one envied by some of my closest friends and people who know me only from Twitter or my website, againstthenumber.com.

What draws people in is trying to find a winner in whatever

games might be played next. That's the door opener, but what intrigues so many are the stories of how the business worked in the old days, including the characters who were involved in paving the way. And boy, let me tell you, there were, and are, some characters.

Most of the episodes in these pages made me laugh when they happened. Some are still a bit painful, but like Alan Alda's character in Woody Allen's classic *Crimes and Misdemeanors* says, "Comedy is tragedy plus time." Enough time has passed that even the most cringe-worthy of my little tragedies are still good for a pained shaking of the head and a chuckle. Hopefully, you'll just laugh.

✎ ✎ ✎

If you're wondering about the title, it goes back to the beginning of the idea for this book.

Gill Alexander has hosted two highly successful podcasts. The first and most popular was "The Betting Dork," which evolved into "The MegaPod." With little marketing or publicity, "The MegaPod" became the third most popular sports-related podcast, behind only Bill Simmons' "The B.S. Report" and Chad Millman's "Behind the Bets," both of which were supported by the media giant ESPN. "The MegaPod" was a gambling round-table discussion with advice on betting football and baseball, depending on the season. The football show, usually recorded on Thursday, was the big attraction. Two regular panelists joined Gill and guest panelists rotated in and out. I was fortunate enough to be a guest panelist a few times.

In 2013, Gill started a second podcast, "Guessing the Lines," in which he partnered up with a Las Vegas betting pro. Gill swore he didn't view the lines until recording time. Then he gave his immediate inclination as to where the numbers would go and which sides might present betting opportunities at the current numbers. Due to some contractual conflicts, the betting pro Gill was working with had to remove himself from the podcast.

Gill and I didn't know each other well until I started my sports-betting company, Against the Number. I'm not sure what he knew about me at that time, but I knew him through his podcasts. In addition, he had a very good reputation for having integrity and brains, not all that common in our business. We had a few Twitter conversations and Gill seemed an even-keeled guy—again, not all that common.

We happened to be in Las Vegas at the same time and arranged to meet. I could tell pretty quickly he was my kind of guy. We talked for the next three or four hours and have stayed in touch ever since. It's not too often you make such a good friend this late in life, but I count him among my closest.

Going to dinner or just shooting the shit, Gill became fascinated by my stories of the old days of Las Vegas and the gambling industry. He asked me if I'd be interested in recording some of those old stories. His plan was to play them at the end of each "MegaPod" show.

When the betting-pro slot opened up on "Guessing the Lines," Gill asked if I'd like to fill the position. He thought I'd be perfect for bouncing his lines off of. For one, I'd been involved in making opening NFL numbers with Roxy Roxborough (we'll talk much more about him further into the book) years before. At that time, Roxy was giving the opening lines to the Stardust and they were considered the "official" openers. I was one of a handful of guys he ran the numbers by before giving them to the Stardust. For another, with my new company, we were using power ratings and other computer-generated algorithms to create lines. It was a commitment, but to do it with Gill would be a real honor. Besides, it would be a great marketing vehicle for Against the Number. We posted both "Guessing the Lines" and "MegaPod" on our website and had an advertising plug for our services on the recordings of both podcasts.

The front segment of "Guessing the Lines" was loose, but informative. Gill actually made his guesses, seemingly off the top of his head, thinking aloud as to what the line should be on each game as we went down the schedule. My approach was much more scientific. As I mentioned, my company had power ratings and algorithms and I had my own personal power ratings. I also reviewed the games well in advance of the show, which we recorded Monday mornings. Gill and my first impressions were often right on and we bragged about tipping listeners off to some winners. It was a solid half-hour to forty-five minutes of information, a good foundation to begin the week for an NFL handicapper.

Once we got through the games, Gill turned the show over to me. My tales of the old days often needed some backstory to set the proper context. Many things were so different in those days, things that young people take for granted, like cell phones and sports books being in casinos. Without the proper set-ups, many of the stories would make no sense. With them, they provided an interesting glimpse into the way this business worked in the past.

So I painted these broad-stroke pictures of how things were. When the interesting part of the story was about to begin, I said, "Then one day ..." I did this subconsciously; I didn't even know I was doing it until after a few episodes, Gill started laughing. "I know the good part is coming," he said.

If you're a fan of 1960s' reruns, the stories unfolded like many episodes of "The Twilight Zone." Everything seems normal, then eventually the main character finds out where he really is: in a human zoo, or back in time, or already dead; some bizarre twist makes him realize all his assumptions have been false.

The stories were so personal to me, I always asked Gill afterward, "Was that okay?" They'd never been told to a broad audience, just a bunch of friends at dinner or a poker game. I had no idea how they'd resonate with the public. But our listeners

4

loved them. The feedback we got was fantastic. There was a lot of it and it was about 99% positive. I remember only one or two dicks who had something negative to say, which is incredible, considering we had so many listeners. I forget how much people want to know what's behind the curtain. I take it for granted, but there's a lot of fascination about the sports-betting industry among highly intelligent and successful people.

My daughter is married to a rocket scientist. People think I'm being sarcastic and he must be a real moron. No. I'm not busting balls here. He actually is a rocket scientist and one of the smartest people I've ever met. One night, I had dinner with him and a few of his friends. These four or five guys were involved in stuff that was so far over my head, trying to learn about it would lose me in about three seconds. I was a bit nervous, thinking back to a line from a "Seinfeld" episode: "Frankly, I prefer the company of nitwits." Meanwhile, all night long, they were the ones who were completely enthralled at how sports betting works. I told them a few stories and they loved them.

After a few episodes of "Guessing the Lines," I was hearing weekly how I had to put these stories into a book. I was skeptical, but after hearing it so often, well, here we are. Several of the stories in these pages were on the original podcast; many more were never told on air for a variety of reasons. I certainly enjoyed telling them. Many others have enjoyed hearing them. I hope you enjoy reading them.

I have to thank Gill Alexander for knowing that people would like these stories, for putting me on his podcast, and for encouraging me to talk about the betting world as it once was. Most importantly, I want to thank him for being such a good friend.

All right, enough with the set-up. Then one day …

Chapter 1

Tark, The Iceman, and Me

I was born into a wiseguy family. My Uncle Jack, whom I lived with from the time I was six years old, was a wiseguy—someone who played every angle he could see and find.

I hate to say he knew every angle, but I wouldn't be surprised if our family tree traced back to Isosceles. There weren't many angles Uncle Jack wasn't aware of.

In those days, when a new Caddy was the coolest thing in the world, certain guys got a new Cadillac every year. Kids today might not get this, but for a generation of Depression Era babies who grew up to be captains of industry, that was one of the ultimate signs of success.

The mobster movies make it look like the wiseguys and heads of the various crime families around the country were getting new Cadillacs every year. That did happen to a certain extent; some underworld guys bought new ones every year. At the same time, they didn't give a shit about a lot of things they probably should have and most of them wound up either in jail or broke or killed. That just wasn't the smart way to do it.

Forget what you see in the movies. Primarily, the corporate execs got the yearly Caddy. They didn't really buy it for themselves, the stockholders did. It was part of their pay package. The board of directors and fellow suits greased the palms of their friends, while getting their own palms greased. Quid pro quo. And you wonder why your IRA isn't what it should be.

If the money was coming out of your pocket, the real bargain wasn't getting the new Cadillac every year. The value was in buying the year-old model. That's what the sharp guys, including Uncle Jack, did.

A new car loses 30% of its value the second it's driven off the lot. Most of the old-time wiseguys who grew up in the Depression weren't going to piss away 30% of the value of anything. Here's where you can make a distinction between a mobster and a wiseguy. Mobsters are doing all kinds of stuff that, thankfully, I don't know all that much about. Uncle Jack was a wiseguy. He bet sports for a living. If you're betting sports, you have to recognize value where others don't. Those habits carry into every aspect of your life. Whether you're buying a car or a cup of coffee, you don't pay more than it's worth.

By the early 1970s Uncle Jack had essentially moved from our home in Pittsburgh to Las Vegas. Even though Pittsburgh was in the beginning of a depression that would last a generation, plenty of corporate executives still got their new Cadillac every year. My cousin Jimmy Manteris, who was a partner of Uncle Jack in their betting operation, was still working out of Pittsburgh. Before he aligned himself with Uncle Jack, Jimmy was in the car business, so he knew all the dealers.

Every year, Jimmy plucked the nicest Cadillac from amongst the year-old models and bought it on behalf of Uncle Jack. The only problem was they had to get the car from Pittsburgh to Las Vegas. Starting in 1973, that charge was given to me, along with Uncle Jack's son, my cousin Zach.

Zach and I grew up more like brothers than cousins. Actually, we were closer than brothers in many ways, because we were only four months apart in age. I still find it hard to believe as I write this, but Uncle Jack had the two of us drive his new Caddies from Pittsburgh to Las Vegas many many times, even though we were still in high school. Our first trip was in the summer of 1973. I turned 17 that April and Zach would turn 17 in August. Yet here we were in a white El Dorado, driving through America's heartland. I can only imagine what was going through people's minds when they saw us in little rural hamlets as we gassed up or got a bite to eat.

We did this every summer and sometimes during Christmas break, if Uncle Jack found another bargain on a car he couldn't resist. But the very first year we drove that car out to Uncle Jack was the most memorable.

Zach and I realized right away that once we brought Uncle Jack his car, we were stuck in Las Vegas with no vehicle. The temperatures were 100 degrees or more (always more) every day, so Las Vegas wasn't exactly a good walking town. Uncle Jack had an apartment near the Strip when that was still a nice area of town to live in. So even though not having a car was inconvenient, two teenagers could find things to do during the day, including hanging out by the pool at the apartment.

Nonetheless, after a few carless days, we got a call from Sonny Vaccaro. Sonny and Uncle Jack were very close at the time. Sonny was originally from Pittsburgh, but was now living in Las Vegas and beginning to gain national notoriety in the world of basketball. Zach and I had also become close with Sonny, working for him in the Roundball Classic he created, traveling to New York with him for the National Invitational Tournament, and going to local high school and college basketball games, among many other things.

"Hello?"

"Chrissy, it's Sonny."

"Hey, Sonny. What's up?"

"I've got a car you and Zachie can use. Are you interested?"

"Hell, yeah, we're interested."

"Okay. I'll bring it over."

A bit later, I heard a knock on the door. It was Sonny.

"There's your car," he said, pointing out to the curb.

"Seriously?" I had to suppress a laugh.

In our world, big fancy flamboyant cars were nothing out of the ordinary. This was an Electra 225, Buick's answer to the Cadillac Fleetwood Brougham. The Brougham was the biggest fanciest car in the Cadillac line available to the general public. Buick was making a play for that same market with this beast and, I have to say, it was doing a pretty good job of it. In fact, Uncle Jack had one himself a few years earlier. This one, however, was a step beyond Uncle Jack's classy Kelly-green model or the white, black, or red you saw ordinarily. The body on this one was an incandescent orange with matching leather seats. Think of the Texas Longhorns or the Tennessee Volunteers team colors. "Subtle" was a word that would never be associated with it. It was perfect for two 17-year-old wannabe Vegas wiseguys.

"George Gervin asked me to watch his car for the summer," Sonny said. "I had no place to put it, so I figured you guys might as well use it for a while."

"Well, geez, Sonny. Thanks."

"No problem. It eats gas like crazy, though. Here, take a couple bucks." He flipped me a $20 bill. (That summer, the U.S. was in the beginning of a gas crisis. Prices spiked from 31 cents to 38 cents a gallon. Sounds like a joke, but I'm serious. People were going nuts.)

Sonny has since become one of the most famous people in basketball circles. He was a marketing executive for Nike, where he signed Michael Jordan to his first sneaker sponsorship. He also worked for Adidas and Reebok and, along the way, became a lightning-rod figure to many. He has inspired much hatred from the sports powers that be and much loyalty from players of all ranks. The NCAA, in particular, has really hated Sonny over the years and campaigned heavily to discredit him, especially after he helped recruit Ed O'Bannon to sue the NCAA over restraint of trade, using the images of college basketball players for commercial purposes without due compensation. NCAA administrators and even some coaches might not like Sonny, because of his evangelistic support of players who he feels have been robbed by the system. I've always said if they could find one player to come forward and talk about how Sonny screwed them, they would love it. They've never been able to find that guy, because he doesn't exist. Believe me, I've disagreed with Sonny on issues many times. But even when I have, I've always kept in mind that Sonny has a heart of gold. I love the guy.

In the summer of 1973, George Gervin was coming off his rookie season with the Virginia Squires of the ABA. He was a good player as a 20-year-old rookie, averaging 14.1 points a game. I knew of Gervin; the previous season, his Eastern Michigan team had played Duquesne, which was my favorite college team at the time.

Gervin wound up having a Hall of Fame career and was named to the NBA's 50th Anniversary All-Time Team. He became known as the Iceman for his cool demeanor on the court. Zach and I had a blast driving the Iceman's car around Las Vegas that summer. Even in Las Vegas, the Tennessee Vol-orange Electra drew stares from people, who were probably expecting scantily clad women with big hair getting out of the car. Instead, it was two teenage boys in cutoff shorts and T-shirts. We fought over who got to drive whenever we went somewhere, which was usually McDonald's or Burger King or to shoot hoops, unless Uncle Jack invited us to have lunch with him and some of his buddies at whatever restaurant they were meeting at. On plenty of occasions, it was just the two of us driving around for the hell of it, with no place in particular as our destination. Spending Sonny's gas money, we often drove around with the windows down, the air on full blast, and the stereo, a great one by 1973 standards, cranking out loud rock 'n' roll.

It's hard for Las Vegas newcomers to believe, but only about 120,000 people lived in the whole valley—Las Vegas, North Las Vegas, and Henderson—at that time. There was no Summerlin, no Green Valley. Boulder Highway was a desolate link to Boulder City and the dam. Rainbow Boulevard was the western edge of the city. The Strip looked nothing like it does today. Most of the places I remember are completely gone. We could take a couple laps around the whole town by the time our day was done. It was great.

About this time, the UNLV Runnin' Rebels had hired a new head basketball coach, Jerry Tarkanian. Sonny Vaccaro's battles as an enemy of the NCAA were nothing compared to what Tarkanian was in for. Tark's war began at Long Beach State, where he was 122-20 in his five years at the Southern California school. He went on to spend virtually his entire adult life fighting the NCAA, eventually winning a $2.5 million judgment against them in 1998.

The NCAA was as corrupt as all institutions become over a period of time. The reason they hated Tark so badly wasn't the fact that he broke all their rules. Everyone, and I mean *everyone*, did. Tark just did it out in the open, brazenly. A lot of coaches act like they have halos around their heads. Tark never tried to fool anyone. And for that, they vilified him.

Big things were expected as he arrived in Las Vegas. His first squad at UNLV went 20-6 while relying heavily on new recruits and transfers.

One of Tark's favorite lines was, "I love transfers. They already have their cars paid for." Of course, the NCAA doesn't allow their student-athletes to have cars paid for by the school. But spend some time on any major college campus with an NCAA tournament-worthy basketball team and tell me what you see. Tark was the only one who admitted it.

If we thought about it at all, Zach and I figured we'd have the use of the Iceman's car until we had to go back to Pittsburgh. We usually stayed in Las Vegas for about a month until we headed back home for the rest of the summer. The time was getting close. It was always with mixed emotions when we left Las Vegas. We were really beginning to love it there.

Then one day … I got a phone call. "Hello."

"You Jack's kid?" asked a vaguely familiar voice on the other end. No niceties were added to the question at hand.

"Yeah."

"This is Jerry Tarkanian. Sonny told me to call you. I need the car."

"Uhm, well, uhm …"

"Here's the address." I wrote it down. "Bring it as soon as you can. We're waiting."

"Uhm …"

"Don't worry, we've got another car for you." He hung up.

Fuck. I sure as hell didn't want to give up that day-glo-orange Electra. Something told me whatever car Tark had to give me wasn't going to be anything like the one we'd been driving.

When I got to Tark's, he was there with a few really tall guys, all in their late teens or early twenties. My powers of extreme deduction led me to conclude this was the UNLV basketball team.

"Okay kid," Tark said. "Give me the keys."

Tark handed them to one of the guys, a kid just transferring into a budding major college basketball program from a small-time junior college. The recruit looked at me and smiled like it was Christmas morning. "Thanks, man."

Tark looked at him. "You'll drive Gervin's car until George gets back from Europe." Then he glanced over at me. "And you'll drive his car." He pointed to this green piece of shit in his driveway. I have no idea what make or model it was. Trust me, it wasn't a Rolls or a Bentley.

I stared at Tark with a you've-got-to-be-kidding-me look on my face.

The whole team was getting a pretty good kick out of this.

Tark slapped me on the back. "Listen, kid," he said. "Look at it this way. You got to drive George Gervin's car for a month. You can't complain about that, can you?"

No. I knew Tark was right. I couldn't complain about that. But goddamn. I was already missing that car.

The piece of shit was our ride for only a few days. I barely remember it. Uncle Jack got us a free trip on a junket shortly after and Zach and I were headed back home to Pittsburgh.

But by then, Las Vegas was in our blood. The pathway of our lives was being laid before us.

Chapter 2

Growing up Greek

In 1922, there was some bullshit between the Turks and the Greeks. If you want more details, look it up; this isn't the place to give a history lesson. Suffice it to say, this was actually a major event in the history of modern Greece and it had a big effect on my life, even though I wasn't born for another thirty-four years. The windup of the skirmish was that all the ethnic Turks living in Greece were given free passage back to their home country. Likewise, the ethnic Greeks living in Turkey returned to their homeland. Sounds nice, but it was also, "If you're Turkish, get the hell out of Greece," and "If you're Greek, get the hell out of Turkey." Call it a post-war, semi-peaceful, ethnic cleansing.

I'm Greek, so I'm not sure exactly how it worked for the Turkish people, but for the Greeks, it was no bargain. Greece was a poor country and now had to absorb about 900,000 refugees. The Greeks who were thrown out of Turkey (oh, sorry, I mean "exchanged," the official word for it) had to leave everything behind or piece off the border guards to enable them to flee the country. Any wealth or even modest assets were left behind. Thus, the 900,000 refugees, my maternal grandparents among them, came to Greece with virtually nothing.

A lot of them, rather than settle in Greece, took off for other parts of the world. There was a huge migration at this time to America, Canada, and Australia. After a brief stay in Greece, my grandparents came to America. After arriving through Ellis Island, they landed in Pittsburgh.

My grandparents had two children before leaving Turkey, a twin boy and girl. While my grandparents were still in Greece, their daughter became ill and died. She was a few months old. During the passage to America, their son became ill on the boat just a day or so out of port. He passed away before they hit Ellis Island. The first thing my grandfather had to do upon his arrival in America, not knowing a word of English, was to find a Greek Orthodox priest in New York and bury his son.

Outside of Ellis Island were agents of different ethnic backgrounds representing various industries and regions of the country, offering jobs to the newly arrived immigrants. I'm sure at least a share of them were unscrupulous characters, but from what I can tell, my great uncle had already been in America for about a year and steered my grandfather, my Pappoú, to an honorable agent. This man directed Pappoú to the small town of East Pittsburgh, Pennsylvania. As the name suggests, East Pittsburgh was about 10 miles to the east of Pittsburgh proper. Westinghouse had built an immense manufacturing plant on 40 acres there, with more than two million square feet of floor space. The Monongahela Valley was the primary heavy-manufacturing area of western Pennsylvania.

All the streams and creeks that feed into the three main rivers that converge in Pittsburgh created numerous little valleys that cut into the plateau where the city was situated just west of the Allegheny Mountains. Separate little towns grew up in each valley, most of them segregated by the various ethnic groups that settled in the Pittsburgh area. East Pittsburgh was one of the main Greek towns of the eastern suburbs.

Our family name in Greek is Φρανζίς. The best English translation would probably be Franzis. However, my grandparents could hardly speak a word of English. In a town of all Greeks, that wasn't such a big problem. Pappoú and Yiayiá (my grandmother) had four more children once they immigrated to Pennsylvania. Filling out the birth certificates, they told the doctors the family name was Φρανζις.

"How do you spell that?"

"Phi, rho, alpha, nu, zeta, iota, sigma, of course."

What could the doctors do? They took their best shot.

As a result, the four kids wound up with three different last names: My Uncle Nick was Frangis. My mother (Mary) and her sister (Christine) were Frangy. My Uncle Jack was Franzi. (I can't get it confirmed, but I'm pretty sure the same doctor delivered my mother and my aunt, resulting in them having the same last name.) The Greeks, of course, stuck with the original Greek pronunciation, but in school and around the English-speaking community, the family name was known as Frangy.

At the start of World War II, my Uncle Nick enlisted in the Army. It was a surprise to him that his legal last name was Frangis. He'd always assumed it was Frangy. When my Uncle Jack joined the Merchant Marines, he found out his legal last name wasn't Frangy, either. It was Franzi. Both sons started going by their legal names. Both girls soon got married. My Aunt Chris married Nick Manteris and my mother married Andrew Zenuh; naturally, they both took their new husbands' last names. So the accepted American family name, Frangy, was pretty much gone.

Some of my very distant relatives in Greece spell our last name with a tau (t) in the middle: Frantzis. That "tz" sound in Greek can sound like a "j" in English. As we were researching family roots, we found out that one copy of my grandfather's Ellis Island papers had his name listed at Franjis. In all honesty, that is probably the name that would be closest to the Greek pronunciation. That makes four different legal spellings of the same last name.

World War II ended and the country started changing rapidly. Televisions were introduced into homes, cars were more readily available, travel was much easier, urban sprawl and the rise of the suburbs were in full force. Factories and their employees thrived in manufacturing centers like Detroit, Cleveland, Chicago, and Pittsburgh. American industry was booming. The middle class and the American Dream were the envy of the world. More kids than ever before had the opportunity to play sports and even go to college with a scholarship if they were good enough. With the added leisure time of the burgeoning economy, people demanded more entertainment. Watching pro and college sports was a natural. Sports flourished as much as any other facet of the changing landscape. Betting on sports, even though it was illegal, started to get a foothold, too.

Bookmakers started springing up around the country. New York and Chicago had the most, but most major cities were doing good business, like Detroit, Los Angeles, and Boston. Some other spots a non-betting historian might not know about, like Kansas City, St. Paul, Minnesota, Covington, Kentucky, and Hot Springs, Arkansas, also booked a lot of action.

From my vantage point a couple decades later, it looked like all the important people doing big sports-gambling business around the country were from one ethnic group or another. I think all the guys I knew in the business were Greek, Italian, or Jewish, with an occasional Irishman and a few other Eastern Europeans. I remember a couple Albanians, Polish, Serbs, and so on. Not one was your ordinary white-guy WASP. The one exception was Southerners. I read recently where some sociologists have now said American Southerners are the first real ethnic subgroup the United States has ever produced. Hell, I could have told them that years ago.

My point is all these groups were largely discriminated against or dispossessed in one way or another. These were the first and second generations of the 20th century immigrants. They were often segregated in their own communities, left to their own little ethnic subcultures. They eventually assimilated fully into society, but it took awhile. They didn't have the same opportunities as those whose ancestors came over on the Mayflower. Pittsburgh had more of these self-contained ethnic sub-groups than any other city in the country. And East Pittsburgh, with its strong Greek community, was one of the prime examples.

A lot of the products of these communities became entrepreneurs of one kind or another: dry cleaners or florists, contractors or housepainters. One kind or another could also find himself with a business that was just this side of the law. That's where my family came in.

✎ ✎ ✎

My own story really begins with my Uncle Jack's story. It was his decision as a young man to get involved in betting sports. Without that, I'd probably be a stockbroker or sports writer or, God forbid, a lawyer.

I have to steal a line from Tina Fey. At least she's a Greek, so I don't have to feel too bad about it. In her book, *Bossy Pants,* she describes her father as being "somebody." I can't think of a better way to describe Uncle Jack. He's *somebody.* He just is.

You can call it *je ne sais quoi* if you know French, which I don't, but it applies here. Robert Pirsig called it "quality" in *The Zen of Motorcycle Maintenance.* Whatever it is, it's there. You can't put your finger on it, but it's what makes Alec Baldwin a star and Billy Baldwin a stiff. It made the Beatles legends and the Dave Clark Five a trivia question. Whatever *it* is, my uncle has it.

I remember once, Uncle Jack and I and a few others were out of town and went to church—it's a Greek thing. We were dressed nicely, my uncle in a classic dark-blue suit and tie. (He's an immaculate dresser. I didn't pick up that part from him.) Afterward, while we were still in the church talking to a few people, a lady took me aside.

"Do you know that man?" she asked, pointing at Uncle Jack. She'd seen us talking.

"Yes, he's my uncle."

"Is he a senator or something?"

I could see why she would think that. He's the kind of man who commands respect. Why? Beats the hell out of me, but there's no mistaking it. He's not big, about 5'10" and 165 pounds; he does have a strong deep voice (that I did inherit), but he doesn't have to speak to get that respect. I got to see it all firsthand.

I've heard a story about my uncle from a couple different sources. I bet it's mostly true.

In the '70s, two separate bettors were robbed and murdered as they came home from cashing out their winning bets at Las Vegas sports books. Each had made a few stops to redeem their tickets, so it wasn't easy to figure out who had been involved in committing the murders themselves or fingering the gamblers for someone else to do the dirty work. The most likely guilty parties were ticket writers or cashiers who worked in the sports book and could identify whoever might be carrying some serious cash.

One particularly big bettor believed he had it narrowed down to two possible guilty parties. He met with a few of his closest colleagues, Uncle Jack being one of them, to see how to handle this. I imagine the scene was probably similar to something you'd see in the movies.

This guy was a little rough around the edges, to put it mildly. His suggestion was simple: Kill them both. A few of the men began to nod in grudging approval. After all, any one of them figured to be the next to be killed.

But before the matter went further, Uncle Jack claimed veto power. A moment before, it seemed like those in the room, all powerful men who weren't afraid of taking the law into their own hands, were about to agree to kill the two suspects. When Uncle Jack spoke, he changed that direction. These were hard men, who weren't ready to play games with their lives, but my uncle still held enough weight to command the room, or at least sway them away from some pretty drastic action. Those two men probably don't know the who, what, or why, but they have Uncle Jack to thank for their skin. They were about to be murdered in an act of vigilante justice. By the way, at least one was innocent.

Maybe both, who knows? Though I doubt it.

Instead, it was strongly suggested to these two men that they leave town. They did. The holdups and murders stopped.

Uncle Jack is now in his 90s. I saw women—young good-looking women—blatantly coming on to him while he was well into his 80s. It's amazing.

I had a longtime relationship with this woman and to call it rocky would be like saying the Sahara Desert is a bit sandy. One day, Uncle Jack was up at Lake Tahoe for the weekend. My girlfriend and I drove up from Reno to meet him and his date for dinner. He was about 70 at the time and the young lady he was with was an extremely beautiful 35-year-old. Driving home, my girlfriend broke up with me. (We broke up about 30 times.)

Why? I wondered. This was about breakup number 10.

"Because you're just like him. And when I get old, you're going to dump me for some young thing."

Obviously, that breakup didn't take. We had a lot more to go before one finally did. But I have to say I was very pleased by hearing her say that I "was just like him." A few other people over the years have said I was like him. Believe me, I'm not. I wish I were. Just being compared to him is an honor.

I don't care if you're talking about a senator, a president, or even a king. Captains of industry, doctors, lawyers, whatever, no one has my respect like Uncle Jack. In *The Godfather,* the book, not the movie, Mario Puzo describes Vito Corleone (I'm paraphrasing), saying he let no one dictate to him how he would live his life. That's Uncle Jack. Of course, he never did a lot of the things Vito did, but he also created a life for himself with his own rules. If he did things that were illegal, they were legal in most of the world. It was only the politicians who made them illegal—until they figured out how to get their piece of the action, even proudly promoting the very things they once prosecuted people for doing. There's legal, then there's moral and ethical. Politicians make things legal or illegal, but people decide what's moral and ethical. Morals can be debatable, but you'll never find a more ethical man than Uncle Jack. You could never live in his world and ascend the ladder to the top by being anything else.

Saying essentially that at a hearing in front of some of those politicians got me in some pretty big trouble once.

✎ ✎ ✎

By the time I was born, the East Pittsburgh of my parents' youth and early adulthood was starting to dissolve. A lot of the Greek families moved up the hill and to the west, to Forest Hills. The same Westinghouse Company that had built the huge facility in East Pittsburgh owned a big block of the eastern end of Forest Hills. The plot of land was essentially rural until after WWII. My Uncle Nick remembers going to the "farm" before it was developed into the neighborhood in which I grew up.

Still, it was totally ethnic, not one WASP to be found. It wasn't all Greek, but there sure were plenty of our people. Within a few streets were the Manteris, Papadopoulos, Stavrakis, Kutlenios, Koutavis, Semetsis, Karastynos, Bargas, Contouris, Carolis, Sorounis, Sklavos, and Poulos families, just to name a few. The rest of the neighborhood was populated with Irish, Italians, and Eastern Europeans. I never met a Protestant until I got to junior high school.

One funny little thing I remember. I was in sixth grade and had to do a report of some kind. It involved a profile of the American population. I was looking something up in the encyclopedia and it said that about 78% of Americans were Protestants. Now, I was worldly enough, even at 12, to know the Greeks were a minority, but I thought for sure the Catholics were the majority in this country. After all, the whole neighborhood that wasn't Greek or Russian Orthodox was Catholic. Well, that and two Jewish families.

I showed it to my father, saying the encyclopedia had to be wrong. Most Americans certainly were Catholic. Right? I can still see my dad, smoking a cigarette, reading the newspaper, and laughing. "Do you think the whole world is like our little neighborhood?"

Well, yeah. Of course I did.

✎ ✎ ✎

My father, Andrew (Andy) Zenuh, wasn't Greek. He was Russian. Even though he was Orthodox, it was still somewhat scandalous in the Greek community when my mother married him. It sounds pretty funny now, but that tells you how life was in the world my parents grew up in. I have pictures of their wedding, which almost no one attended. Even my grandparents, Pappoú and Yiayiá, refused to go. Of course, my dad was such a great guy, they soon made up. Yes, Greeks can be a little hot-headed and irrational at times. Years later, when my grandparents were in failing health, my father had an addition built on our house to give them a place to live. Pappoú and Yiayiá loved my dad.

As a Russian Orthodox, my dad didn't have to convert to attend Ypapanti, the Greek Orthodox Church in East Pittsburgh. His former Russian Orthodox Church was around the corner and I think he went occasionally with his father, but he became an active parishioner and board member of Ypapanti.

I found out as a teenager that my father wasn't born Andrew Zenuh. He was born Andrew Russnak. His mother was a Russian immigrant and from there the story gets a little murky. One version has it that she and my biological grandfather were married, but he contracted influenza soon after my father's birth (1912) and passed away. Another version is my father was born out of wedlock and my biological grandfather abandoned mother and child. Knowing the times, I have to give a little more credence to the second version, but I honestly can't be sure. My grandmother then married George Zenuh, another ethnic Russian who immigrated to this country from Czechoslovakia. My father never knew his real father and always considered George to be his dad, biological or not.

My grandfather's last name when coming through Ellis Island was spelled Czenyuch. It underwent a few changes, too, before the family decided on Zenuh as the spelling. Russians use the Cyrillic alphabet, as you no doubt know, so the translations can be as haphazard as Greek names. Add one more crazy spelling story to my family history.

I was never all that close with my father's side of the family. It's not really anyone's fault, it's just that I was so close to the Greek side. Had I known then the Russians would be the new organized-crime kingpins of the American underworld, I might have embraced my Russian heritage more strongly as a youth. I'm joking. Mostly.

My father grew up in a small hillside town between East Pittsburgh and Forest Hills, Chalfant Borough. It's almost completely Eastern European. While East Pittsburgh was a happening place, Chalfant had a few bars that were pretty much places just to get drunk. With an abundance of alcoholism in the Eastern European community, my father's side of the family had its share, too. My dad wasn't an alcoholic, though both his half-brothers were. I was very fortunate not to inherit that gene. By the way, I'm now 62 years old and don't think I've ever met a Greek alcoholic. We drink plenty in our culture, but there's a big difference between drinking and becoming an alcoholic. I've heard the reason there aren't many Greek alcoholics is that wine was present so early in our culture that the gene petered out; enough of those who had it died before they could pass it on to the gene pool. I'm not an anthropologist, but it makes sense.

I played Little League and Pony League baseball in Chalfant, so I did get close to some of those kids, but I never got very close to the only two male cousins I had on that side of the family. Instead, growing up in the more Greek community of Forest Hills and going to the Greek Orthodox Church in East Pittsburgh, I grew closer to my Greek side, even though my father was very close with his family.

When I was 14, my father died very suddenly from a massive heart attack. I was done playing baseball at that point, so the Chalfant connection disappeared. Once I had children of my own at 28 years old, I decided to change my last name. Since my father wasn't even born with the last name of Zenuh and I wasn't close with that side of the family, I honored my father by taking his first name as my last. Instead of Andrew, I added the "s" and made it Andrews. Since Andrew was my middle name, I also added Zacharie as my middle name to honor Uncle Jack (his legal name), who became a second father to me after my dad passed away.

✒ ✒ ✒

When I was about seven, Uncle Jack and his wife divorced. While it's commonplace now, divorce was almost unheard of in 1963. Uncle Jack got custody of the kids and moved into our house with the two girls. His son, Zach, moved in with my aunt and uncle down the street, the Manteris family. However, after a year, Zach also moved in with us. In our pretty small four-bedroom two-bathroom house were my mother and father, my Yiayiá and Pappoú, Uncle Jack and his kids Zach, Cindy, and Olivia, and I. It probably was a little weird to some of the other families in the neighborhood, but it was normal to us.

My Pappoú died that year after a fairly lengthy illness, so eight people in the house dropped to seven. That's the way it stayed until my father passed away in 1970.

I was born in April 1956. My cousin Zach was born in August 1956. As I've mentioned, we were in many ways closer than brothers. We remain so to this day. He was best man at both of my weddings and I was best man at his. We rode the same bus to the same school, had the same friends, played on the same sports teams, and went to the same church, besides living in the same house.

My other cousin, Art Manteris, whose house Zach had originally moved into, lived less than a mile away. Art was born in June 1956—three of us born in a four-month period. He also went to the same school, had the same friends, played on the same sports teams, and went to the same church.

It was a great childhood. But in some ways, for a kid, it was no bargain. Between my father, my Uncle Jack, and my Uncle Nick (Art's father), the three of us had three fathers. Throw in my mother, my Aunt Chris, and Yiayiá and we had three mothers, too. We couldn't get away with anything. Any and all weren't afraid to punish us. Art's two older brothers and sister wouldn't hesitate to kick our asses either.

When Archie's (that's Art's nickname to friends and family) brother got married, his wife said, "You guys are one big extended-immediate family." Yeah, that about nails it.

Still, it was great growing up with essentially two brothers the exact same age. We did a lot of things together.

I don't know if it's nature or nurture, but we all ended up in the gambling business. My cousin Archie is now the Vice President of Race and Sports Operations for Station Casinos. Before that, he had similar positions at Caesars Palace and the Las Vegas Hilton (now Westgate Las Vegas).

My cousin Zach has been a professional bettor for many years, but now has a job on the other side of the counter, running the Virgin River and CasaBlanca sports books in Mesquite, Nevada.

Of course, we got an early start to our gambling and book-making careers. When we were in fifth grade, we started copying Uncle Jack's sheets with the football lines from all over the country. We either got up early in the morning or waited until he went to the bathroom to get the numbers for all the games. Then the three of us each made about 10 handwritten parlay cards and distributed them to our classmates. We never got caught, but if we had, we should have gotten into trouble for larceny, not bookmaking.

We put up all even numbers and ties lost (a huge advantage for us). We used little tricks; a favorite was -7, but the underdog was +6, or -11 and +10. Since ties lost, you were always laying or taking a half-point worse than what was on your ticket (a player lays points when betting the favorite and takes points when betting the underdog). Pick 'em games (a 50-50 coin flip, with neither a favorite nor an underdog) were -3 on both sides. All that added up to a monstrous edge for us as bookmakers.

If you don't remember or probably weren't born, in the mid-sixties, the Steelers were the worst team in football and while we were booking parlay cards, the University of Pittsburgh had three straight 1-9 seasons. Almost every kid in class had at least one of the local teams on their cards.

We weren't exactly generous with our payouts, either. We booked only 3- and 4-teamers. A 3-teamer paid 3-1 and 4-teamers paid 5-1. In case you aren't aware, typically, 3-team parlays pay 6-1 and 4-teamers pay 10-1. Good Lord, we were crooks.

Believe it or not, the two years we booked the cards, fifth and sixth grade, not one of our customers had a winner. Never once. We sweated the cards in fifth grade, but by the time we got to sixth grade, we just figured if anyone ever claimed to win, we would go back and check to see if it was true. We never even had a claim.

We had to learn our lessons, though. Back in those days, not many college football games were broadcast on television. If you were lucky, you got two games on a Saturday, but usually it was just one. Some little networks (what guy at my age doesn't remember Jefferson-Pilot broadcasting games?) had games on independent stations. There weren't many of those either. We would get most big games, like UCLA and USC or Nebraska and Oklahoma, but you might go years and never see teams like Oklahoma State, Iowa, or Washington.

When we did have a game on television, it was automatic; we were watching it. About that time, the local PBS station, WQED in Pittsburgh, showed games on Tuesday night. We saw teams from the Deep South, like Grambling and Alcorn State. Sometimes they showed the Ivy League or other teams from the Northeast.

I'm not positive which game it was, but I do remember the pointspread. For the sake of the story, let's say it was Lehigh vs. Lafayette, two teams that were on quite often. I remember I liked the favorite, let's say Lehigh.

I'd been talking about it for a few days leading up to the Tuesday broadcast. On the day they were showing the game, Uncle Jack took me aside and asked me if I wanted to bet on it. Sure, I said. After all, I was a gambling man, even at that age. We dickered over the number and eventually he got me to bet Lehigh -21½ (Lehigh had to beat Lafayette by at least 22 points).

Sometime before the game, unbeknownst to me, he also took his son Zach aside. Zach liked the underdog and Uncle Jack knew it. He asked Zach if he, too, wanted some action on the game. Of course he did; Zach is as much a gambling man as I am. After some dickering, they arrived at their number. Zach had Lafayette +20½. Now if the game ended exactly on 21, Uncle Jack won both bets.

For the better part of two years Zach and I had been watching these Tuesday night games, which were broadcast in their entirety, with halftime marching bands and the whole thing.

Then one day ... *that* day to be exact, we noticed a splice in the game, which cut out a little time. We looked at each other in amazement. The game was taped! We didn't know!

"What did you take on Lafayette?" I asked Zach.

"Twenty and a half," he said. "What did you lay on Lehigh?"

"Twenty-one and a half," I answered. "Holy shit. Your dad screwed us. This game's coming twenty-one!"

We ran to find Sunday's paper and sure enough, Lehigh won by 21.

When he got home that night, we said, "We aren't paying. No way. You knew the score."

"Bullshit," Uncle Jack said. "If you let me past post you (betting after a game has started or with the outcome already determined) by three days, you deserve to lose. You two geniuses even looked the game up in Street and Smith's and said they had the game listed for Saturday, but thought they made a mistake."

I'm pretty sure I was the genius who said that.

"Now go get me your money."

Zach and I each lost a dollar that night. Actually, we each lost $1.10. He made us pay the juice (the amount a bookie charges above the base amount of a wager that's retained on losing bets, in this example, the extra .10), too.

We did learn a couple of valuable lessons, though. First, don't get past posted—and definitely not by three days. Secondly, don't take the worst of a number, especially a key number. There's a huge difference between 20½, 21, and 21½. We lost about a week's worth of profit from our parlay-card operation, just because we were too stupid to know the right day of the game.

Damn!

✐ ✐ ✐

Both my cousins were athletes. I wasn't. Oh, I tried, but I had no talent. Archie was a pretty good baseball player. He was the starting second baseman for our high-school team, then went on to play junior-college ball at Boyce Community College.

Zach was one of those guys who do could anything, even

though he was pretty scrawny all the way through high school. During our senior year, it was discovered that he had a heart condition. He had to restrict his cardio after that, so he turned to weight lifting. A year or so later, he'd gone from about 145 pounds to close to 200. All muscle. He got cleared afterward to play basketball again, which was his number-one sport.

By that point, he was in his second year of college, so his chances of getting a scholarship were pretty much gone. But he did play on our church team.

Like most loosely organized church teams, we had a bunch of guys who might or might not show up. When all our guys showed, we were good. Our front line was 6'8", 6'7", and 6'6". The smallest of those three was Al Mallah. He went to Greece and had a very good career in the Greek professional league. I still see him listed as one of the all-time greats in Greek basketball history.

We had a couple different shooting guards, of whom Archie was one. Zach was our point guard. Not many 6'0" white guys could dunk in the mid-'70s, but Zach was one of them. Besides being our point guard, we often put Zach on the other team's best player defensively. He could guard the point with his quickness or muscle a bigger guy underneath enough to keep him off the block with his strength. With that team, we won two pretty big tournaments.

I say "we," though I already told you I wasn't very good. The only way to get your name in the scorebook was to score or foul out. My chances of scoring were dismal at best. So I came in off the bench and did my best to foul out as quickly as I could. When you're trying to foul out, it's amazing the stuff they *don't* call. What are you going to do? Complain to the ref that you hacked the guy and he missed it? No. I'd just try to foul him harder next time.

Then one day … we went to the Detroit tournament.

The Detroit and Chicago tourneys were the big ones. Both

cities had huge Greek populations with lots of Greek Orthodox churches nearby and an abundance of church-sponsored teams. Naturally, plenty of teams in the Midwest and Great Lakes region wanted to come in, take down the local team, and go home with a trophy. Some of the best Greek teams and players in the country showed up. There were always a few guys who were college players. Some, not many, were Division I, and a few more were from basketball's lower divisions.

Add to it that we didn't have all our guys. In fact, we hardly had any of them. One of our big men, not Mallah, showed up, and Zach and Archie. Not many of our key bench guys were there either. In other words, we had no shot.

We were paired up against a team from somewhere in Ohio. They had one guy from a small Ohio college who was about 6'7" and could score. If you're 6'7" and can score, you're going to kick some ass at a church tournament and that's what this guy was doing.

Toward the end of the game, this guy had a shitload of points and his team was killing us. He'd fouled out our whole front line by then and we were pretty much playing the scrubs, including me. Meanwhile, this big guy was still in the game.

When the last of our big guys fouled out with less than two minutes to play, the coach told me to guard their big guy. Now, even though I didn't have much talent, I wasn't bad playing on some short hoops in a driveway. My shooting range was about three inches, but I knew how to get leverage underneath. I could get position and keep it, so if I could somehow get the ball, I could score. I fancied myself a big man in a six-foot-tall body. I always thought if I could have been six-ten, I could have been … well, to be honest, I could have been a six-ten bookmaker. But I sure as hell would have been a lot tougher in a church league.

The coach had me playing center, so on offense I went underneath on the left block, more to stay out of the way of the rest of the offense than anything else. One of the kids playing guard fed me the ball while I was standing there with my back to the basket, like a classic center. Their big guy was on me like I was some kind of threat. I figured, what the hell, we're already getting killed, how much worse could I make it? I dribbled across the lane, stuck my left forearm in the big guy's chest, pushed him back to create some space, and shot a sky hook Kareem Abdul-Jabbar would have been proud of. Swish.

"That's a foul! That's a foul!" the big man was yelling at me. "You pushed off!"

Now, I'm not the most confrontational guy in the world, but I sure don't like eating a lot of shit, either. "The ref was standing right there and he didn't call it. So it's not a foul."

Running down court, he shouted, "You pushed off!"

I'd had it at this point. "Fuck you," I said. "Why are you even still in the game? You guys are up by thirty-five and you have at least thirty yourself. You should be ashamed of yourself."

He started screaming at his point guard as he set up underneath. "Give me the ball! Give me the ball!"

He had rage in his eyes like Charles Manson on a meth runner. I knew he wanted to get the ball and dunk it right over me. And if he could bowl me over, that would be even better. He wasn't much concerned about getting a charging call in the process. He really wanted to kill me.

Like I said, I didn't have much talent, but growing up in my household, I knew as much about the game as any 20-year-old. I had pretty good timing, too.

He got the ball and as he came around with it, he held it right in front of me, just like I knew he would. I came down hard on him with my right hand. I didn't mind hammering him at that point, but I actually got all ball. It bounced hard off the floor and back up to about chest level. I could see the panic in his eyes as he tried to corral it, gather himself, and jam it in the hoop and down my throat at the same time. Instead, he fumbled around for it until it squirted off his hands and trickled out of bounds.

The ref grabbed the ball and made the call. "Off you," he said pointing to that big asshole. "This way," and he pointed our way.

I looked over at our bench and my two cousins were on the floor and I'm not exaggerating: They were on the fucking floor laughing their asses off. We held the last possession and took some final shot and that was the game.

We lost by 35 and were dying laughing. They won by 35 and I thought their big man was going to start crying. When it comes to bragging in my athletic career, that's it. That's the highlight. A 35-point loss by my team, but at least I made their star player cry.

✐ ✐ ✐

Our next tournament was in Chicago. All our guys did show up for that one, but I couldn't make it; I was back in Pittsburgh, working at CJ Barney's Wooden Keg bar.

During one of the games, Zach stole the ball off the point guard and was on his way to a breakaway dunk. He planted his left foot to take off and his knee collapsed. He tore his ACL and both MCLs. Even with today's medicine, he would have been out a year. In those days, surgical procedures weren't nearly as good. They fixed his knee, but he never again had the same flexibility in his leg. He still played ball, but he was never close to what he'd been.

Due to his injury, Zach went back to weight lifting and he turned into a monster. After we moved to Las Vegas, he finished second two years in a row in the Mr. Nevada contest. He never took a steroid, although all the other guys did. If he would have taken them, he probably could have competed in even bigger contests. Rather than get into all that crap, he gave it up and went into the business of owning a gym.

He's well into his 60s now and still looks like Hercules.

Chapter 3

Indicted, Innocent, and Immigrated

A watershed event in 1970 changed the course of our family's history. Fortunately, it wasn't a tragedy, but it was life-altering for all of us.

At the end of the 1960s, the world was going through some dramatic changes. You know, all the major stuff: civil rights, Vietnam, the counterculture. The isolation of little towns similar to where my parents had grown up was quickly vanishing. People were spreading out, moving to the suburbs and out of big and small cities, just like my parents had done. Telephones and televisions were in every house. The world was closing in on these tiny ethnic enclaves.

Many legally questionable activities that had been overlooked, unknown, or implicitly approved, sometimes with the help of payola, by local law enforcement were now coming into the harsh glare of state and federal spotlights. Police protection in some little town was barely an annoyance to the FBI.

Then one day ... my Uncle Jack got indicted.

And not just indicted, they threw the book at him. Across the street from the entry to the massive Westinghouse factory, Uncle Jack had a little candy store. Behind the store was an anteroom where he was writing business. Bookmaking business. He gave out betting slips, just like they did in Las Vegas. The standard order in most small-town candy stores was "a Milky Way and a Tootsie Roll, please." In Uncle Jack's store, it was "a Hershey bar with almonds, the Steelers plus six to the Colts minus three-and-a-half parlayed for twenty bucks, and a bag of M&Ms." He was booking business all those years with a nod and a wink (and I imagine a nice little envelope) to the authorities. No one really gave a shit.

He made some money out of the candy store, but he was making real money from his betting. In those days, small bettors went into little bookmaking outfits like Uncle Jack's, while the bigger players were doing business on the phones. Uncle Jack was a real player. A lot of those calls wound up being made interstate, which is how the FBI got involved. Interstate gambling is a federal crime.

When the news broke, it was huge. The authorities and the media painted Uncle Jack as a major underworld figure. Remember the various names my family had wound up with? Here was where it came into play.

One local news show had a graph, listing on the vertical axis Uncle Jack's name with three "aliases": Jack, which the whole world knew him by; Zacharie, his legal name; and Zach, which no one in the world had ever used in referring to him. He was Jack, never Zach. Some legal documents had his name as Zacharie, just like if your name is Bill, while your driver's license has William. No one might have called you that, other than your parents chewing you out. It doesn't make it an alias.

Most rational people would probably have been able to see through the first-name fallacy, but then the news station listed the three last names as aliases on the horizontal axis: Franzi, Frangy, and Frangis. I can still hear the news anchor reading all nine permutations, "Jack Franzi, also known as Zacharie Franzi, also known as Zach Franzi, also known as Jack Frangy, also known as Zacharie Frangy, also known as Zach Frangy, also known as Jack Frangis, also known as Zacharie Frangis, also known as Zach Frangis, has been indicted on charges of interstate gambling, racketeering, money laundering, and other organized criminal activities."

I imagined some sweet little old lady sitting at home and listening to this. Of course she would think Uncle Jack was the Greek version of John Dillinger or Al Capone.

The FBI followed Uncle Jack for about 18 months. At the hearing, they presented pictures of him at basketball and baseball games, often with Zach and me by his side. We'd gone to the Final Four that year in College Park, Maryland. We went to the NIT that year, too. They had pictures of those trips, which somehow were supposed to be evidence of his underworld activities. They had pictures of us out to dinner, playing miniature golf, bowling—hell, doing everything a normal father and his sons might do.

They also had our phones tapped all that time, with reams of transcripts for every conversation that took place in our house. Uncle Jack was pretty careful to use payphones when possible, but the FBI put two and two together and came up with some references to games that were bet or going to be bet or had been bet.

I was 14 years old and my parents now had a transcript of every telephone conversation I'd had for the past year and a half. Remember, kids, this was long before cell phones; we all shared the one house phone. (Actually, I think we had two: You know, business.) There were no texts or emails. No Twitter or chat rooms. No playing Words with Friends and using the message function where you might think your conversations are private. None of that. Every conversation with our friends that wasn't in person was on that goddamn tapped phone. When this came to light, Zach and I just about shit our pants.

Uncle Jack had the boxes of the transcripts in the cellar of the house. Zach and I snuck down there to read as much of these things as we could. How is a 14-year-old supposed to remember what he said to one of his friends on the phone more than a year ago, or even a week ago? We needed to get our stories straight if things came down, which we figured was inevitable.

YiaYiá's conversations were really funny to us. Naturally, they were all in Greek. Seeing how the FBI transcribed this stuff was hilarious.

We saw a lot of other stuff, too, that we couldn't help but read. At that age, we were a lot more worried about getting in trouble ourselves than we should have been. We were worried about Uncle Jack, too, believe me, but we mostly wanted to see what anyone could get on us. We also wanted as much dirt on my cousins Cindy and Olivia that we could use later on.

For months, we lived this case daily. For the first few days after the indictments came down, it was *headlines,* but long after it faded from public view, it was never far from our thoughts. There were constant calls from Uncle Jack's lawyers. Friends called occasionally, but came by the house even more often. In this world, friends, real friends, showed their support. One thing I learned first-hand is that it's the tough times when you realize who your friends are. Uncle Jack had some good ones.

At school, it was pretty big news, too. Most of the kids from the neighborhood already knew what Uncle Jack did, so that really didn't change much in our relationships with the local kids. We were in junior high now, though. Our world had expanded a little. We were in good with the kids we cared about, but a few kids were warned to stay away from us. And they did. The teachers gave us some curious looks, too. Who knows what they thought?

I'm not sure exactly how long the trial lasted, but it wasn't long. The judge quickly threw out the case for a variety of reasons.

When I said the feds threw the book at Uncle Jack, I meant it. But they should have thrown more like a pamphlet at him. The book they threw contained so many things he didn't do, the judge couldn't take any of the allegations seriously. Uncle Jack later admitted that if they'd just stuck to what he actually *did* do, they might have won their case. Other than handling the penny-ante stuff at the candy store, Uncle Jack was never a bookmaker. He was a bettor. While betting across state lines was and is illegal, it's slap-on-the-wrist illegal. Bookmaking is different. Right or wrong, the feds see bookmaking in a whole different light. I'm just guessing, but I think they see it as more like a conspiratorial organized-crime thing. I guess you can ask your friendly FBI agent if you really want an answer.

The prosecutors had Uncle Jack as a ringleader of this vast bookmaking operation. It simply wasn't true. He was just placing bets with the bookmakers. The FBI and the prosecution really didn't understand the difference.

That wasn't the main thing that killed their case, though. I don't know how the law works today, but back then, for the cops to wiretap someone, a judge had to approve it.

The judge could authorize it for up to two weeks at a time. After the two weeks, the cops had to present the evidence. If the judge believed there was enough evidence to continue the wiretap, he could authorize it again up to another two weeks. The burden of proof was on law enforcement. It was just like innocent until proven guilty.

The FBI, the top law-enforcement agency in the land, was conducting the investigation. They got authorized for the first wiretap, presented their evidence to continue, got it reauthorized, presented again, and got it reauthorized again. But that was it. They never went back again to get it reauthorized. They had 18 months' worth of wiretaps, and their whole case depended on it, but only six weeks of it was admissible in court.

The judge looked at all the pictures they had of Uncle Jack, too. Zach and I were in at least half of them. While the FBI was trying to show what a criminal Uncle Jack was, it showed more of what a family man he was—out to dinner, at ball games, just a regular guy. And there were Zach and I, barely into our teens, alongside.

Of course, we knew what was going on with his gambling, but I imagine if you're reading this book, you don't have a moral problem with making a bet. I sure don't. And by the way, neither does the government. What Zach and I were learning was how to do it the right way. It did a lot more for my future and my career than anything I ever learned in school.

Uncle Jack had his son and his nephew and he was probably smart enough to know that they figured to follow in his footsteps in one way or another. I'm not trying to make the guy out to be Jesus or even a saint, but he was a definitely a family man and he had our best interests in mind. And even though he was a second father to me (my real dad was still alive), he became the best second father you could imagine.

Hearing friends of Uncle Jack describe it, it sounded almost as if the judge laughed the prosecution out of court. He didn't, of course, because at the core he was incredulous that the top law-enforcement agency in the country, or in the world as they'd like to have you believe, could so callously ignore the law.

I suppose many, or maybe even most, people have events in their lives that greatly shape their future. This was mine. I know now, first-hand, how the truth can and will get manipulated.

The prosecution accused Uncle Jack of everything they could think of. They wanted to paint him as the worst criminal they could to get the judge and jury to convict this accused linchpin of a top-crime syndicate. Maybe they were playing poker, hoping he'd plead down to lesser charges. Whatever it was, they had their own agenda—of which truth and justice had no part. They wanted recognition and promotions just like everyone else in every other walk of life. Problem was, they were looking to get it by hanging someone's scalp on their belt.

After the dust settled from the case, Uncle Jack knew that Las Vegas was the only place for him. He could do all the betting he wanted where it was completely legal.

✐ ✐ ✐

My father died in October 1970. By 1975, my mother had moved to Las Vegas, too. In 1977, Zach and Archie moved out there to finish their college degrees at UNLV. Archie's parents and his sister's family had moved out there already.

I finished my degree at Robert Morris in Pittsburgh in 1978. After graduating *cum laude* with a degree in business administration and just shy of a double minor in accounting and economics, I had a few interviews lined up. I went to the first interview and canceled the rest. I couldn't see myself in the corporate world, working 9-5 and wearing a tie every day. Besides, Pittsburgh was in the throes of a terrible depression at the time. The steel industry was quickly vanishing, while the whole region relied on steel production. Its collapse sent ripples through all of western Pennsylvania, where decent jobs were just about non-existent. Certainly, no good ones were available for young college graduates.

So I was tending bar at the time and thought I'd keep doing that until I figured out what I wanted to do. I was making good money as a bartender, booking a little on the side, and partying pretty hard. I was on a bad track and didn't realize it.

Then one day … I was closing down the bar and talking to a couple girls. Archie was in town and it looked like we were in with these two. I'd just scored an ounce of pot and we were heading back to my apartment to party. They were following me in their car and I had a new (used) car I'd bought off Uncle Jack. It was 2:30 in the morning and the streets of Pittsburgh were empty.

While these girls were following me, one thing led to another and we started racing home through Oakland and up Squirrel Hill on Forbes Avenue. There had been a light rain that night and as the road swung to the right, my car fishtailed and we hit a telephone pole. I've made some stupid moves in my life, but that has to rank in the top two.

Fortunately, only the back of my car hit the pole after spinning a 180. Archie and I weren't hurt, by some miracle, but the car was totaled. I'd had it for about three days. I slipped the ounce to the girls and told them to get lost before the cops showed up. Believe it or not, I wasn't drinking. I was just being an idiot.

The next day I had to call Uncle Jack and tell him I'd totaled the car.

We knew a guy who was flying junkets from Pittsburgh to Las Vegas and he was flying out the next day. Uncle Jack put me on that flight. I flew to Vegas, met him at the deli where he chewed my ass out in front of a bunch of his cronies and bought me lunch, then he sent me back home on the next flight out. God's honest truth. I made a round trip between Pittsburgh and Las Vegas in one day just to get yelled at. In a Greek family, you never outgrow answering to your elders. At least the lunch was pretty good.

Meanwhile, I realized it was time to start making my way in life. That meant leaving Pittsburgh, where there was virtually no opportunity, and moving to Las Vegas, the fastest growing city in the country. Then I could go full-time into the business I'd prepared for my whole life.

I missed Pittsburgh. I miss it still. But I guess things worked out pretty well for me. There are always sacrifices to be made and leaving Pittsburgh was something I really didn't want to do, but felt I had to or I'd be stuck in a rut there forever.

I packed up and left. I arrived in Las Vegas with a full tank of gas and everything I owned in the trunk of my car. I had a quarter, two lousy bits, in my pocket. I'm not bullshitting in the least. I had a place to stay with Uncle Jack, but that was it.

Time to figure things out.

🖋 🖋 🖋

Las Vegas is about 90% transplants. Reno has a lot less, probably about 50%. These are just my guesses, by the way. In either city, a big question is, "What brought you to Nevada?"

When you're a sports book ticket writer, just working the counter like any clerk anywhere, no one really cares. Even when you're a sports book manager, it's not such a big deal. But later, when I was important enough to attend political dinners and charitable fundraisers and award ceremonies, I answered with, "In 1970 my uncle got indicted for bookmaking and after he beat the rap, we came out here where the family business was legal."

It was a great test of character for anyone who asked. I got some great looks, especially from the Nevada natives, born in the state, who not so secretly think everyone who comes here is some sort of carpetbagger. On the other hand, this is Nevada, after all. A lot of people thought it was hilarious and loved it. The ones who were appalled made it even more fun.

🖋 🖋 🖋

About 25 years after he beat the indictment, Uncle Jack, Zach, and I were out to dinner in Las Vegas. A guy came up to our table and asked, "Are you Jack Franzi?"

"Yes."

"You won't believe this, but my first job out of law school was working for the FBI. I was assigned to your case. I was one of the guys listening to your phone calls. I was writing down the sides you were playing and calling my bookie when I got off work. It was the best two football seasons I ever had!"

We laughed our asses off. It turns out that old FBI agent was a great guy. He was just a kid doing his job.

And the Puritans want to put bettors in jail. What a joke.

Chapter 4

Stardust Memories

Every successful person has at least at little good luck at some point. I had a really lucky break soon after I arrived in Las Vegas. In the summer of 1979, I got hired at the Stardust race and sports book.

In case you aren't aware, the movie *Casino* is based on the Stardust from right around the time I worked there. You might have seen the movie. If not, it's definitely worth a couple hours of your time. Even though I was just a kid in my early 20s, I was about to get the education of a lifetime. I got to witness a lot of what *Casino* was about firsthand.

The movie centers on action from before, during, and after my time there. Lefty Rosenthal ran the whole casino for the Chicago mob. Tony Spilotro was the mob's muscle guy. In the movie, Lefty, played by Robert DeNiro, is known as Ace. Tony, played by Joe Pesci, is Nicky. Just before I got to town, the Nevada Gaming Control Board, the state regulators of the casino industry, forced those two and some of their close associates, including the guys running the sports book, out of the joint.

Uncle Jack was bitter enemies with the guys who just got tossed out on their asses. But he was good friends with the guys who took over the book afterward. So, like the way a lot of things work in Vegas, I had Uncle Jack to juice me into the job.

Almost all the names used in this chapter have been changed

to protect the … well, you can't call them innocent. Rather, they're disguised to protect *me*. That's a lot more accurate for my motives. Everyone knows Ace and Nicky were Lefty and Tony. If they're public figures, I don't mind using the names, especially if they're no longer among the living. Otherwise, just assume they're all phony.

I was originally hired to write horse bets in the race book, but I was told that once football season came, which was only a few weeks away, I'd be switched to sports. That was perfect for me, because I wanted to learn as much about the race and sports book business as possible. At this point, I knew almost nothing about the horses. I learned a little about booking races and a lot about reading a *Daily Racing Form* and picking winners from those guys at the Stardust. Believe it or not, that was pretty good for me personally. I'm pretty far ahead of the horse-betting game over my lifetime. I'm one of the few guys in the world who can say that.

When I got switched to sports, I was low man on the totem pole, so I had to work the graveyard shift on football weekends. After I was hired, one of the other joints in town closed up and two of their guys, both in their 40s, were hired on at the sports book and placed above me. I completely understood. First of all, both of them were way more experienced than I was. Second, they were Italian. That's just the way the joint worked; it was almost like my old neighborhood back home. You had to be Italian, Jewish, or some other non-WASP to work there. A lot of the bosses were from Chicago, so being Greek didn't hurt. If you don't know, next to Athens, Chicago has one of the world's largest Greek populations in the world. Many of my country-men had been involved in the betting and bookmaking racket in Chicago, just like everywhere else they settled. Only two regular white guys worked in the whole sports book. They both had some larceny in their hearts, though, so they fit in perfectly.

Undoubtedly, there's a ton of bullshit about "men of honor"

and the romanticized movie version of wiseguys, but without question, they take care of their own. Guys who were out of work and needed jobs were put to work. Most of them weren't really needed in the positions they were hired for, but they still got taken care of. Also, if a player was busted out and needed a meal, the bosses made sure he got a ticket to the buffet. It's all different now with the suits running the joints. I'm sure Wall Street and middle America find it much more palatable, but it was way better back then. Especially for guys like me, with good connections.

My first day in sports, they threw me right onto a betting window at midnight. I opened up and started writing tickets. It was the opening week of football and we were jamming. The one other guy working next to me was an Italian from Chicago, recently fired from some other sports book. We wrote for a half-hour straight before we got to the end of the line of bettors. We hadn't even been introduced yet.

This guy looked over at me. "Kid," he said. I thought he was going to shake my hand and tell me his name. "There's only one thing in the world better than a thirteen-year-old."

"Yeah?" I replied. Where the hell was this going, I wondered. "What's that?"

"Two thirteen-year-olds."

Welcome to the Stardust sports book, I thought.

There I was, my first night on the job, working for 30 minutes next to a guy who turns out to be a pedophile on the hunt for teenage hookers. Jesus. I thought being raised how and where I was had completely prepared me for this. I was wrong. And I hadn't seen anything yet.

There was quite the cast of characters at the Stardust sports book. Between the guys working behind the counter and the customers, I didn't know which were worse. That's not to mention the mob guys still running the entire operation. I was in for some kind of education. And not the kind you get at Harvard.

47

✏ ✏ ✏

I'd been at the sports book a few weeks when the two guys I mentioned earlier from the closed sports book showed up for work. One of them, Frank, was put on the graveyard shift with me. We ran graveyard only on weekends during football season, so it was always busy with an array of drunks, creeps, and weirdos who were around Las Vegas in the middle of a Saturday night in those days.

Then one day … about three in the morning, things had finally settled down. Frank told me he was going to take a walk.

"Sure," I said.

He disappeared for about 20 minutes and came back, his face white like freshly cleaned linen.

"What is it?" I asked. I thought he might be having a stroke or something. He had black hair with graying temples and a bald spot on top. He was about a hundred pounds overweight with an open shirt revealing a collection of gold chains atop a chest with hair so thick, it could swallow a golf ball like the rough at the U.S. Open. Central casting couldn't have found a better character.

"I went for a walk," he said. He bent over, trying to catch his breath. "I went out to the parking lot."

"Yeah?"

"You aren't going to believe this …"

"Yeah?"

"I swear to God, I saw a fucking elephant."

"You saw an elephant in our parking lot?"

"I swear to God, I saw it. I swear. I must be losing it."

"Frank," I said. "It's the elephant from the show, Lido de Paris. They walk him every night through the parking lot to give him his exercise."

"Oh, thank God," he said, letting out a deep exhale of relief. "I took a Quaalude. I thought I must've got some bad shit."

✒ ✒ ✒

As low man on the ladder, I had some shit duties to perform every now and then. On those graveyard weekends, my shift started at midnight and I didn't get off the next day until the 10 a.m. game went off in the morning. Then I had to run out and get sandwiches for the crew. We had a standing order at this Italian restaurant for egg, pepper, and pepperoni sandwiches. Jesus, they were good.

Meanwhile, by the time I put in my shift, counted out my drawer, ran for the sandwiches, then stayed to eat while mine was still hot, I was putting in 12 hours. That's not so bad, as long as you're getting paid for it. But that's not the way it worked. You got paid by the shift. Once again, these guys really did take care of you. But you had to pay your dues first. It was some kind of rite of passage and I understood that. I was 23 years old and a ways off from earning my stripes, juiced into a job or not. On the other hand, the guys who'd been around were putting in five- and six-hour shifts and getting paid for a whole day.

It started pissing me off.

Then one day … I couldn't keep my mouth shut anymore. "Robert," I said to my boss, "it's not right that I put in twelve hours and not get paid overtime. I see these other guys working half that time and getting a full day."

"Listen kid, the joint doesn't pay overtime."

"Well, that just isn't right."

"You think they're gonna change the whole system because of you?"

"No …"

"Well then, keep your mouth shut."

"Yeah, but …"

"You know you started at forty-five a day, when everyone else starts at forty, right?"

It was true. I did start at forty-five bucks a day, five bucks

49

a day more than everyone else—Uncle Jack's juice, once again. I was reminded of it every so often.

"You know," Robert continued, "you're a smart kid. You got a good future in this business. Just do what you're told and you'll be fine. Come baseball season, you'll have days where you'll be out of here on a short schedule and get paid for the day."

I shrugged my shoulders. I knew he was right.

"Listen," Robert said, "if it really bugs you, take a hundred out of the drawer every now and then. No one gives a shit."

This was my boss. Yep, the Stardust was one hell of a joint.

🖊 🖊 🖊

Though I moved to Las Vegas when I was 23, my name had been known throughout the betting community for a few years prior to that. "This one is for Chris" was a sort of code for one of the city's top handicappers giving out his best NFL play of the week.

As popular as it is today, HBO was a fledgling network in 1977. It was developing its own programming as it delved into its limited movie library. One of its programs featured legendary bookmaker Bob Martin giving the opening NFL line to two handicappers, who bet into the line. Bob then adjusted the line accordingly before making it available to the public. At the time, Bob was working at the Union Plaza (now the Plaza) in downtown Las Vegas, the first casino to host a race and sports book, after developing his reputation as the world's top oddsmaker and bookmaker at the Churchill Downs sports book.

For those of you who are unaware of Las Vegas history, Bob Martin was the Babe Ruth of the bookmaking industry. Others were more famous in the media, but real handicappers and bettors had no doubt about the one and only authority.

Martin grew up in the Brownsville section of Brooklyn. An avid Dodgers fan, as a teenager, he started betting on them in pool halls, then booked his own prop bets from his high-school buddies. He raised his action, and level of sophistication, in the Army during World War II; he returned to the States with a $30,000 bankroll and became a bookie in New York and D.C. In 1963 at the age of 45, he moved to Las Vegas where sports betting was legal. He started there as a bettor, but after a few years was hired by owner Harry Gordon to manage his new book, Churchill Downs. There, his posted numbers on games became known as the "Las Vegas line," which was used by bookmakers all over the country.

Nowadays, you hear about the opening number, but whose opening number? Some Las Vegas sports book? Some offshore gambling operation? Sure, any one of those could be legit. But back in the day, the opening number meant one thing: Bob Martin's opening number. No one else's mattered.

From Churchill Downs, Bob moved to the Union Plaza. His long-time friends and associates Johnny Quinn and Jackie Gaughan built the downtown hotel-casino in an effort to offer what they envisioned as a true competitor to the Strip. Part of their business plan was for Bob to run the biggest and best sports book in Las Vegas.

Enter HBO. The young cable network reached a deal with the Plaza to televise Bob opening the NFL line with veteran sportscaster Tom Kelly as the host. The first year, the featured handicappers were Bobby "the Tower" Berent and Lem Banker, two of Las Vegas' most respected football bettors. Lem had a rough season and was replaced the following year by Larry Merchant, a veteran writer and boxing analyst.

Bobby Berent was nicknamed the Tower because he owned the Tower of Pizza restaurant on the Strip. (The restaurant was a solitary building where Park MGM stands now.) Bobby was also a partner of Uncle Jack's for many years. While he was Bobby the Tower to most people, he was Uncle Bobby to me.

I'd known Bob Martin and Bobby Berent since I began

visiting Las Vegas as a 14-year-old in 1970. They were two of Uncle Jack's best friends. I had lunch at the Celebrity Deli or dinner at the old Venetian restaurant on West Sahara with those Hall of Famers and others for years. I was smart enough to keep my mouth shut and my ears open and learn as much as I could from the absolute best in the business. They were all a bunch of characters, but Bob Martin was one of the funniest men alive and a real ball buster. I knew I could joke with him, because he could take it and give it back in kind.

Very few people had cable television in 1977 and even fewer had HBO. My cousin Jimmy was the first person we knew who had both. A crew of us gathered at Jimmy's house to watch the opening-line show every week.

During one episode, Bob Martin said, "I know we have a lot of fans in Pittsburgh who watch the show every week. I want to say a special hello to Jimmy Manteris, Johnny LaGorga, and Frankie Zemmarelle."

The next day I talked to Uncle Jack over the phone and told him to tell Bob that if it had been Uncle Bobby saying hello to the fans in Pittsburgh, he wouldn't have left me out. Of course I was kidding, busting balls, and Uncle Jack, Uncle Bobby, and Bob Martin all knew it. I mean, I was 22 years old, a year out of college, still tending bar, while Bob was 60, on TV, and a legend. To be serious, it would've been like a guy trying to make a Rookie League roster talking shit to Babe Ruth.

On the show the following week, Bob Martin said something to me on the air, busting my balls right back, as was his way. Later in the show, Bobby Berent told Bob that since he forgot me the previous week, he was going to make this week's best bet "for Chris."

His bet won easily and a new tradition was born.

Every week, Bobby announced his best bet and said, "This one is for Chris."

I was betting on all of Bobby's picks, but I always put a little extra on his picks "for Chris." I don't remember what his record was, but I sure won a bunch, pressing my bets the whole way.

By December I was playing pretty high, especially for a 22-year-old bartender. I was up to $200 on some of my bigger plays.

During the Week 14 show, when Bob Martin got to the Seahawks-Browns game, before he gave out the line he said, "I have a feeling this one will be for Chris. I make the Seahawks minus three over the Browns."

"I'll take Cleveland plus three," Uncle Bobby said immediately. "I like it, but this one *isn't* for Chris. I'll have another game later."

Bob Martin rarely gave his opinion on a line he'd just made. This time, however, he did. "Did you hear that, Chris? Cleveland plus three. That is *not* for you."

I'm no idiot. This was Bob Martin telling me, and anyone else who was smart enough to read between the lines, that he liked Seattle in the game. That was about as close as I'd ever come to hearing God speak directly to me through the prophets. I made the biggest bet of my life on Seattle, $500. The Seahawks exploded, taking a 23-0 lead and winning easily, 47-24. There was no way I should have been betting a nickel a game, but I walked away with an easy win.

Within a few months, I made the decision to move to Las Vegas and, as you know, by the next football season, I was writing tickets at the Stardust. Bob Martin's show had been cancelled by then, but I was still getting games from Uncles Jack and Bobby. Plus, I was getting great numbers—as explained later in this chapter, I got the shaded lines (a line that's been altered to create a better bet) that the preferred customers at the Stardust were getting. And I got to see some of the sharpest players around betting at the book. Life was pretty good.

Then one day ... one of our sharpest players was chatting with me at the window. I'd gotten to know him pretty well that football season. "I sure miss Bob Martin's show," he said. "I loved getting the games from Bobby the Tower, especially the ones for Chris."

"Yeah," I said. "It was pretty cool, him giving me those games."

"Wait a second." He looked at me, looked at my nametag, and looked at me again. "You're *Chris*? *That* Chris? I had no idea. I figured it was some old Jewish guy from Pittsburgh."

"No, it was me."

He told a handful of the regulars. For the next couple weeks, I had guys coming up to me, incredulous that I could possibly be "Chris" from the TV show.

Even years later, while I was working in Reno, I got an occasional "You're *Chris*? From Bob Martin's TV show?"

Yep. It was me. That was how I became a well-known celebrity in the world of Las Vegas sports betting before I was anything but a snot-nose wannabe wiseguy.

✐ ✐ ✐

The Stardust Race and Sports book was crawling with every kind of character you could imagine.

The race book had overhead projectors displaying the day's races with the horses' names, the jockeys, and the odds. The room was set up like an amphitheater, with semicircular rows of desks for the handicappers to look toward those projected displays and point them toward the ticket writers. It was state-of-the-art for the time, but almost comical now. Races weren't shown on television and we thought we were in the modern ages by getting race re-creations from the wire service. The joint was filled with cigarette smoke that wafted to the high ceilings and hung like an overcast sky about to let loose a thunderstorm.

The sports book didn't have much room for sitting. They wanted guys to make their bets and get the hell out of there.

There were only a few televisions, which made sense; not many games were televised. We got the games of the week in the major sports and the rest of the scores came in on the "ticker" (tickers, telegraphic machines that printed out data on a strip of paper, especially stock-market information or news reports, were common in those days). No one complained that much about the lack or speed of information. Why would we? We didn't know any better. You kids don't know how good you have it.

It seemed to me like every guy in the Stardust had some sort of scam going. I remember one guy selling pirated VCR tapes. Another guy was married to a hooker and was looking for guys to pay him for an hour with his wife. There were strippers and poker players, who fit together well—being the blackest-hearted people in Las Vegas. The guys directly in the sports business were by far the most honorable. Most were either booking themselves or servicing a bookmaker from back home by giving them the Stardust line. Some were trying to hustle a buck betting and middling games (betting both sides of a contest at different numbers with a chance of winning both wagers). There are always scumbags in any profession, but for such a collection of anti-social misfits, everyone got on pretty good.

Except for one family. We called them the Mansons. The father, mother, and son were all drug dealers. I think they imported cocaine, but I didn't want to know too many details about these people. Few of us working there did. I do know they were creepy. And as you can imagine, they had money to burn. They sure burned a lot of it betting sports at the Stardust.

The dad hardly ever said a word. Nonetheless, you could tell he was not the kind of guy whose bad side you wanted to be on. The thing I remember about the mother was her constant complaining. She bitched to us about the lines, the TVs, the air-conditioning, the pager system. She bitched about the valets. She told us how lousy the food was or how the shows were no good, being comped to everything, too. When we paid her for a winning ticket, she complained that the bills were too old or too new. I'm not kidding, this woman could complain about anything.

And what do you think happens to a kid being raised in that environment? I don't need to do any experiments to make a reasonably sized bet that the kid will be pretty screwed up. And he was. The son, Keith, was about 25 years old and looked like the kind of guy who played linebacker in high school. He wasn't big enough to play college football, but he was pretty thick through the shoulders and looked like he could take care of himself. He tried to be friendly to those of us behind the counter, laughing and spewing a few wisecracks, but he could turn in a flash.

The guy selling the pirated VCR tapes got into a fistfight with him once in the casino. It was definitely Keith who instigated it, but nothing happened to him. He and his mom and pop were there the next day like it was nothing. The Manson Family obviously had some sort of juice, but again, I didn't want to know too much.

One of Tony Spilotro's closest people was Lenny, who was always around. One of the muscle guys, he was *very* scary and that's putting it about as nicely as you can. We knew there was no messing with Lenny, but we all still liked him.

Then there was Dave, a really bright guy, who was the main handicapper for Spilotro's group. If he wasn't well-educated, he sure seemed like he was. He wasn't just brilliant with numbers, he also knew the arts, politics, and current events. We talked sports and betting, but also music, movies, books, comedians, that sort of thing. Dave and I became pretty good friends when he discovered I knew Mars Bonfire, and not John Kay, like most folks believe, was the original lead singer of the band Steppenwolf. I always wondered how he fell in with these guys. But when Dave bet, we were told to take care of him. He automatically got a point the best of it in football and basketball and a break in the price of any baseball bet.

A Point Better

Back in the Stardust days, giving an extra point to a good or otherwise influential customer wasn't that uncommon. It might not have been a completely kosher business practice, but it wasn't technically against any regulations. An extra point in basketball, where the numbers all have similar value, would raise the player's win percentage by 2%-3%. The value varies in football, depending on the number (taking +4 on a bet that should be +3 would be huge, while taking +9 on a game that should be +8 wouldn't mean nearly as much).

Years later, Nevada Gaming instituted a regulation that a line had to be available for anyone to bet it, meaning you couldn't offer a deal to just one person. It might be done on occasion today, but it's definitely against gaming regulations.

Dave was a little guy, about 5'6" and maybe 135 pounds. I'm not positive of his age, but I think he was a lot younger than he looked. He looked 45, but I think he was closer to 35.

Without knowing or wanting to know too many of the details, it seemed like all the guys in Spilotro's inner circle were Italian or Jewish. Lenny, Dave, and the Manson Family were all Jewish. I'm not sure what it meant, but it seemed to mean something at the time. Like I said, these weren't the kind of people of whom you wanted to ask a lot of questions.

Then one day ... I was sitting at my station and I saw Dave and Keith talking. They were in the middle of the sports book, about 20 feet from me. Nothing seemed amiss. Suddenly, Keith launched an attack on Dave, bloodying him and knocking him down, and maybe out, with a combination of three or four punches. Lenny was at the counter, about five feet from me. About the time Dave hit the floor, Lenny was all over Keith. It was the most brutal beating I've ever seen a man take. Lenny had Keith on the floor pounding his face with a series of punches before taking a bite out of his cheek. The other guys, including security, were standing around not knowing whether to break up the fight or not. It reminded me of the scene from *The Godfather I* when Sonny was beating Carlo with the garbage can.

While all this was going on, Dave was lying on the floor, semiconscious and bleeding. I locked my drawer and went out to help my friend. I picked him up and took him into the bathroom, wet some paper towels, and cleaned him up. After a few minutes, some of the boys from the outfit came in and took him from me. He was still pretty groggy, but they had hold of him and carried him out.

By the time I came out of the bathroom, the fight was over. Keith was on the floor looking like someone put a hand grenade down his shirt. Lenny was still steaming, but left, catching up with the guys taking Dave out of the joint. No cops were called and no one else ever got involved. Things were kept pretty much in-house, but the Manson Family wasn't around much after that. We saw them occasionally, but they must have found somewhere else to hang out. I know they were still in town for a while. A few years later, the dad was taken to the hospital and passed away there. Keith, being the less than rational person he was, rammed his car through the lobby doors. Accounts vary after that, but I'm pretty sure he shot up the place, too. He did some serious time for that one. I'm not crazy about locking people up, but this guy shouldn't have been anywhere near other human beings.

The next day I was working my usual shift. Lenny came up to the side of the counter and called me over.

"Hey," he said, holding out his hand with a few hundred-dollar bills in it. "We want to thank you for helping our guy."

I don't want to pretend I had any experience or was so street-wise that I knew exactly how to handle this, but I did know a couple things. First one is, you don't really want to get involved with these guys. Once you're in, there's no easy way out. On the other hand, you don't want to insult or piss these guys off, either. On the *other* other hand, the money was definitely tempting. I was making $45 a day and looking at a couple weeks pay. All I had to do at that point was shake the guy's hand.

"I wouldn't feel right taking it," I told Lenny. "I don't want to make it like I did anything—other than just helping Dave because I like him." I still wasn't sure how this was going over. "I hope you understand. I don't mean any disrespect."

"Are you sure?" When he gave me a look like, that's fine, I started feeling all right with things.

"Yeah," I said, "I appreciate it, but it just wouldn't feel right."

"Okay," he said, and that was pretty much the end of it.

After that, he started coming to my window with all his plays. Keep in mind, this wasn't some regular customer. I remember once the Steelers were -10½ over someone.

"We're taking the Steelers minus seven for thirty-thousand."

"Uh, you know I have to get this okayed, right?"

"Yeah, yeah, do what you have to do. But we both know what the outcome is going to be."

And we did. I went to tell Robert about the bet and he just shrugged his shoulders. "It's their money. What are you going to do?"

That's the way it worked. Lenny came to the window, usually mine now that he knew I was all right, and told me the game they wanted and the price they wanted it at. I could always tell how good things were going by how much they moved the line for themselves.

Sometimes a game was -4½ and they'd tell me they were

laying three. The next game was -4½ and they laid 1. Meanwhile, all they ever seemed to do was take the favorite. If they ever did take the dog, they wanted to pad the shit out of the line, 3 points the best of it at a bare minimum.

Lenny was the one who would come in with the big money. That was besides what Dave was playing, while getting at least a point on every game. He only bet a few dimes a game, though. Sometimes they actually middled games right at the window. Lenny told me they were laying 2½ and taking 4 on the same game on two consecutive tickets. The middles players scoured the Strip and downtown trying to do the same thing, while these guys did it in a matter of seconds. God only knows how much they were taking out of the joint.

Spilotro's crew wasn't the only beneficiary of the Stardust bosses' largesse. As far as I was personally concerned, they took good care of me, too. It wasn't outright robbery, but I sure hit a pretty high percentage of my plays. Robert let me play the same number Lenny or at least Dave got, as long as I kept the bet to a hundred dollars. That was not only plenty for me in those days, it was a hell of a perk.

Sometimes I even got better than they did. That Steeler game I mentioned always kind of stuck out in my mind. After Lenny told Robert he was laying 7 when the game was really 10½, Robert asked me, "Do you want a piece of the Steelers?"

"Yeah, sure."

"Write yourself a ticket, Steelers minus six and a half for a hundred."

"So if the Steelers win by six, you want me to lose my bet?" God, I was an asshole. Robert was giving me a half-point better than Lenny got and I still asked for more. He should have decked me.

"Jesus Christ, what the fuck?" he said shaking his head. "Go ahead, write it at minus six."

"Thanks, Robert." I saw him walk away chuckling. I guess

he wasn't too pissed. He kidded me about that one for years afterward.

In many ways, Las Vegas was like the Wild West in those days. Not many episodes exemplify the true character of the growing city like an incident that occurred a few years before I arrived on the scene.

Around 1977, I was hanging out downtown at the Fremont. This was before I moved to Vegas, though I'd turned 21 and was just making the sports book scene.

While I was watching a basketball game I'd bet on, this guy in the back of the Fremont sports book was screaming at everything. It didn't matter what either team was doing, everything was cause for this guy to yell and shake his fist at the TV.

A made basket?

"Motherfucker!"

A missed basket?

"Motherfucker!"

A foul?

"Motherfucker!"

A rebound, a pass, a turnover, a timeout, halftime, whatever was occurring, this guy motherfucked the game.

The Fremont wasn't exactly a high-class joint in those days, or in these days either, now that I think about it. Nonetheless, I was somewhat surprised that no one had any sort of problem with a guy carrying on like this there. Ticket writers, supervisors, customers, security, no one showed any concern. Finally, I went up to one of the ticket writers I knew and asked who that was.

"Oh, that's just Cryin' Kenny," he said. "No one pays attention to him. He's always like that."

Thus I was introduced to this infamous Las Vegas hothead.

I saw Kenny occasionally over the years, though I doubt he

had any idea who I was. After all, I was just one more young jagoff trying to make his way in the business, like a million other guys who come to the desert following the siren's call of an easy life from your gambling winnings. But every sports bettor in town knew Kenny or at least was aware of him. How could you not? Kenny's act didn't play well in any of the Strip casinos; even the Stardust wouldn't put up with him. So Kenny hung around the downtown casinos or the standalone sports books.

And like everyone else in town who knew Kenny, it wasn't long after finding out who he was that I heard the story that made him famous. Or infamous, depending on your point of view.

I wouldn't call Kenny a wiseguy, but he was definitely no square, either. He was a degenerate at heart, but he was sharp enough to be on the right side of a number more often than not. He also bet almost all underdogs and never ever bet a game over. Of course, nothing can break the heart of a gambler like a game being a dead under and it sneaks over by a miracle. You know you have the right side and instead of pocketing your winner, all the squares are cashing their tickets. It can get to the best of us. Then one day … it got to Kenny.

It was Friday, June 4, 1976. The Boston Celtics and Phoenix Suns were playing in the NBA Finals. The series was tied at 2-2 when Game Five came back to Boston. This turned into a triple-overtime thriller in an even series, with the old-guard Celtics taking on the up-and-coming Suns. It was great theater, great drama for anyone with even a remote interest in NBA basketball. If you Google "best NBA game ever," Game Five in the 1976 series will be among the top three.

As thrilling as it was, it was a heartbreaker if you bet the game under at the total of 215. You had a loser, even though you handicapped the game as perfectly as possible. After all, regulation ended with the score tied 95-95, well under the total (overtime counts in the total result).

After the first overtime, the score was tied once again, this time at 101-101. Here's the thing. With seconds to play in that first overtime, the Celtics got the ball after the Suns had tied the game. As they pushed the ball up the court, Paul Silas, one of the Celtic veterans, called a timeout. The trouble was, the Celtics didn't have any timeouts left. In this case, the referees are supposed to call a technical foul. Instead, they ignored both Silas' request for the timeout and calling the technical foul.

The Suns were livid and had a right to be. For years, the Celtics had been accused of getting away with murder for all sorts of rules violations. Whether the past accusations were true or not, this one was blatant. Had the Suns been awarded the single foul shot after time had expired, they very likely would have won the game 102-101. And Kenny would have still won his under bet.

The game went to a third overtime.

The Celtics took a 111-110 lead on a John Havlicek basket with one second remaining. The time keeper let the buzzer go off, signaling the end of the game. Celtic fans stormed the court in celebration. But the refs ordered one second to be put on the clock. The replay shows that this was proper. And then referee Richie Powers was assaulted by a fan. There must have been a full moon that night, because that's far from the craziest thing that happened.

The clock stopped with the Havlicek basket, but the Suns had to take the ball out under their own hoop. Suns guard Paul Westphal convinced coach John MacLeod to call a timeout that the Suns didn't have, to force the refs to call a technical foul on them. This one the refs did call, and Jo Jo White converted to put the Celtics up 112-110. The advantage to the Suns was that after a technical, a team gets to inbound the ball from half-court. Gaining the extra forty-five feet of real estate paid off when Garfield Heard threw in a prayer at the buzzer to tie the game.

The Celtics won by two points at the end of the third overtime, 128-126. The total, obviously, had long since gone over 215.

It was a memorable game for Celtics lovers and haters, a historical note in NBA history, and a heartbreaker for the Suns and their followers. It was also a game that brought about one of the most legendary moments in Las Vegas sports betting lore.

Cryin' Kenny watched Game 5 that night at Bill Dark's Del Mar Race and Sports Book in North Las Vegas. As Roxy Roxborough said after hearing me tell the story, calling the Del Mar a little seedy was probably the nicest thing ever said about the joint. It was the perfect spot for Kenny.

Kenny, of course, had bet the game under 215. Kenny was screaming at everything, everyone, every play, every call, and certainly every hoop. The Celtics got a large dose of his vitriol as they blew a 22-point lead to let the Suns back in the game and eventually tie it to send the game into overtime. Kenny and his under bet survived the first overtime, but when the refs failed to call the technical on Silas at the end of overtime number one, Kenny knew he was dead. Halfway through the second OT when the game finally went officially over, Kenny let fly with one more outburst and stormed out of the Del Mar.

Sometime before the end of the game, Kenny returned. Only now, he had a gun. He walked into the Del Mar, openly brandishing the revolver. The crowd turned its attention from the game to check out the crazed Texan who had madness not only in his eyes, but in his very soul. Everyone who really knew Kenny was aware that as crazy, emotional, and uncontrollable as he was, he wasn't a violent man at heart. The Zenith TV hanging from the ceiling, however, wouldn't concur with that sentiment. Especially not after Kenny lifted the gun, pointed it at the television set, and emptied the six-shooter into the poor innocent collection of wires and tubes. After it hissed and spit, then fell to the floor, Kenny looked around the room in triumph. "That's the last game that'll ever go over on that TV," he proclaimed. He holstered the gun and walked out.

Now it's very possible Kenny might have had a bit too much

to drink the night of Game 5. He was known to have a cocktail or two, or perhaps a bunch more than that. Like many of us who have behaved somewhat poorly after a night of over-indulgence, Kenny came into the Del Mar the next day to apologize to Bill Dark. Bill made him pay for the TV, but Kenny's action (his betting) was welcomed the next day like nothing ever happened. What could you do? It was Cryin' Kenny.

Bill Dark even put a frame around a few of the bullets that had gone through the television and lodged themselves in the plaster. Beneath the framed bullet holes was a plaque, with the following inscription:

June 4, 1976
Cryin' Kenny, under 215
Game 5 NBA Championship Celtics 128 Suns 126
3 Overtimes

Many years later, Bill Dark finally had the inside of the Del Mar painted. He forgot to tell the painters to leave the bullet holes as they were and the monument to Kenny was laid to rest by a can of cheap acrylic house paint.

That indeed was a sad day. I think Roxy is still in disbelief that Bill Dark ever even thought to pay someone to pretty up the place.

Can you imagine if that were to happen today? If Cryin' Kenny had been in the Wynn or the Venetian when a game went over after multiple overtimes and he shot out the TV? The SWAT Team would be called in. The whole joint would be on lockdown. Kenny would be led out in handcuffs (or worse) and looking at doing serious time in the state penitentiary.

Yep. Things were handled a little more casually in the old days.

Meanwhile, back at the Stardust …

In Magic Johnson's rookie season, 1979, it was apparent pretty quickly he was going to be a special player. It was all the more remarkable, because Johnson was only 20 years old, skipping his last two years at Michigan State to join the Los Angeles Lakers. By the end of the season, in the championship series finale, he had a game that is still considered one of his best, even after his career ended years later.

Though Magic was a key player for the Lakers, Kareem Abdul-Jabbar was still the main man on the team. In game five of the Finals against the Philadelphia 76ers, Jabbar had 40 points in the Lakers' win, which put them up 3-2 for the series. But Jabbar severely sprained his ankle in that victory and didn't even make the trip to Philadelphia for Game Six.

The series was seen as pretty even throughout. Each team was moderately favored on their home court and each team had won in the opponents' arena leading up that game. With Jabbar out, the 76ers had gone up to a 9-point favorite, way higher than the line for any other game in the series.

Uncle Jack had me running around and taking the Lakers +9 everywhere I could find it. Usually when Uncle Jack bet, the line moved all over town, but we were finding plenty of what we were looking for. After I checked in with him, telling him what I'd taken, I mentioned that to him.

"Yeah," he said, "I might have moved too early. Lefty's outfit is on Philly. They're laying eight and a half everywhere."

The word was out on both ends. With Uncle Jack taking all the +9s and Lefty laying all the -8.5s, no other numbers were going to show up. No matter what side you wanted, when you saw -8.5 or +9, you had to bet it. The sports books loved it, as long as the game didn't land on 9. With only a half-point of exposure, it wasn't much of a risk to write that much action. We got down a bunch on that game, I can't remember how much, but we needed the Lakers to win outright, or not to lose by 9 points or more, for a pretty big chunk. For Lefty, the Sixers had to win by at least 9 points.

Lefty Rosenthal and Uncle Jack were enemies. I can only speculate why Lefty hated Uncle Jack. Lefty was used to everyone rolling over for him. The only ones who didn't were the deeply connected and potentially violent guys like Tony Spilotro. And my Uncle Jack. Uncle Jack wasn't deeply connected with any mob guys and certainly wasn't violent. Nonetheless, he never rolled over for anyone, including Lefty. Uncle Jack was smart enough to stay away from Lefty, but he'd be damned if he was going kowtow to him in any way, either. Lefty wasn't exactly kowtowing to anyone either. So this was a battle of wills between two very strong men. World War I probably started over something like this.

In case you haven't figured it out yet, the Lakers won that game, and the series, with Magic turning in one of the legendary performances in NBA history: 42 points, including 9 at the end of the game; plus, he made all 14 of his free throws, had 15 rebounds, 7 assists, 3 steals, and a blocked shot, and was named MVP of the series.

Shortly after that, Uncle Jack had me cash tickets all over town and settle up our accounts. But we had a problem. I was $4,200 short.

I counted my cash and my outstanding tickets, backwards and forwards, I don't how many times. Each time it was the same thing. I was short $4,200. I spent two days looking for it. I'd kept good track of every bet I made, every ticket I had, and where I bet them. I kept all my losing tickets until we settled up, too.

That's where I found it.

I had a ticket for $2,200 on the 76ers -8.5. I knew that wasn't our bet, as we only had the Lakers +9. Shit shit shit. I knew I'd been pretty thorough in checking my tickets, but beyond that, I wouldn't even have bet in a book that had the 76ers -8.5 (hence,

Lakers +8.5). Had I seen that number, I would have just walked out. So what happened?

The ticket was at Sam's Town. This was the new hotel-casino on Boulder Highway built by the Boyd Group (years before they took stewardship of the Stardust). What happened was, I didn't bet it.

Sam's Town took bets from Uncle Jack over the phone. Back in those days, that was strictly against Gaming regulations, but people tended to do favors for my uncle, even the pure-as-the-driven-snow Boyd Group. That's the way life worked then and works now. Wiseguys get favors done for them. When I went into Sam's Town, I just handed the guy the money and he handed me the ticket that Uncle Jack had phoned in. It was all done clan-destinely, like I was selling state secrets to the Commies. I never even bothered to look at the ticket. That was certainly my fault. But I'd been given the wrong ticket. That was their fault. Now what? I seriously did not want to screw things up with Uncle Jack.

I went to see the guy who ran the sports book, and there's no nice way to put it—he was completely incompetent.

Next, I pleaded my case to the casino manager. He called down to the sports book to get the manager's side of the story. He was told that they had a $2,200 bet on each side in that game. He also said the other bet, the one on the Lakers, which should have been mine, hadn't been cashed yet. I asked if I could put in a lost-ticket claim on that ticket, but they weren't going for it. They felt whoever had that ticket had paid for it and was entitled to it. It looked like I was stuck. They handed me the wrong ticket and since I didn't catch it, I was out the cash.

Then it hit me. Who else would they write a ticket like that for? They probably wrote it over the phone and handed the runner the wrong ticket, just like they handed the wrong one to me. And who would have had the 76ers -8.5 in that game for $2,200? It could only be one guy. Lefty.

Marty Kane and Joey Boston operated the Stardust sports

book before Gaming ran them out, along with Lefty. They'd been Lefty's right-hand men in the sports business for a while. Lefty may have hated Uncle Jack, but I believe to this day that Marty and Joey only pretended to. I can understand. Lefty didn't have many known enemies, so for Marty and Joey not to go along with him in a situation like this wouldn't be very smart on their part.

While neither of them could outwardly tolerate Uncle Jack, for some reason Joey loved my cousin Zach. I'd only been in town about a year at this point and even though I knew who Joey was, I didn't know him personally. But I knew he loved Zach. I'll say this: Everyone loves Zach. I don't know how you can't. He's the kind of guy that women love and other guys can see exactly why.

I called Zach and explained that I was $4,200 short because Sam's Town had given me Lefty's ticket. He said he'd call Joey and see if there was anything he could do to help. I had to see Uncle Jack in a few hours to settle up, so I was on pins and needles. I sat by the phone waiting for his call.

Brrrrring. I answered the phone on the first ring. "Hello."

"What the fuck is Joey Boston doing with my forty-two hundred?" It was Uncle Jack.

"Um, um."

"Joey Boston picked up my ticket from Sam's Town and you got their ticket."

I knew that already. I just didn't want Uncle Jack to know it.

"Uhm, so, what are they going to do?"

"They found that ticket in Marty Kane's garbage can. He didn't realize it either. Marty is going to give it to Joey and Zach will go pick it up."

"Okay. Well, at least we got our money."

"Why didn't you tell me?"

"I wanted to get it back before you even knew it was missing. I almost pulled it off. How did you find out?"

"Marty Kane called me."

"Well," I said, "considering what happened, I did the best I could."

"Tell me what happened."

I gave him the story.

"And you figured it out?"

"Yeah."

"Well," Uncle Jack said, "Columbo couldn't have done a better job. You did good."

I have to tell you, that was pretty high praise. Uncle Jack doesn't throw it around very easily.

I also have to say, as much as Lefty and his crew didn't like Uncle Jack, they had enough honor to make sure he got the money he deserved. They could have easily cashed the ticket and just refused to pay. Uncle Jack couldn't have done much about it. But between the respect for Uncle Jack and Lefty and his crew wanting to do the right thing, they made the money good. Good on Lefty. There probably aren't many who've said that. But I have to say, thanks, Lefty, Marty and Joey. You guys saved my ass.

✏ ✏ ✏

Things changed in the late 1960s for little towns like the one my parents grew up in. Similar things were now happening in Nevada. The old days of organized-crime syndicates running the casinos were ending. It was really just a matter of time until they had to conform to same rules the rest of the world was following. By the late 1970s and early 1980s, that time had come.

Technically, the Stardust was owned by Argent, a corporation backed by Teamsters money. The Teamsters were backed by some shady money themselves and, well, it's not that hard to put two and two together.

Argent bought the Stardust and that was when Lefty Rosenthal was installed as the casino boss. He had a couple different titles, but everyone knew he ran the joint regardless of what it said on his business card. Lefty had a pretty colorful past (how's that for soft-soaping it?), but he was allowed to operate for a while. Tony Spilotro's past was way too toxic to even give him any air of legitimacy in the eyes of Nevada Gaming, so he was strictly in the background.

In the movie *Casino,* Ace (Lefty) was made to be a good businessman who was rough around the edges, but smart and fair. I can tell you, that wasn't how most people looked at the real Lefty. Most were pretty scared of the guy; they saw him as ruthless. When he was removed by Gaming as the boss, under whatever title it was, he then became the "marketing director." In that capacity, he created "The Frank Rosenthal Show." David Letterman he wasn't, let me tell you. It was awful. However, the biggest names in Las Vegas made appearances on the show: Frank Sinatra, Dean Martin, Don Rickles, Tom Jones, Sammy Davis, Jr., and many more. That's how much juice Lefty had. Not many people would tell him no.

Even though most of the Stardust employees were scared shitless of Lefty, guys like him always have a few fans. A security guard liked to come and talk to me while things were slow during the graveyard shift. With an air of nostalgia, he told me about the days when Lefty ran the joint.

"I liked Mr. Rosenthal," said the guard, who was nice, but not particularly bright. "He treated me just fine."

"Oh yeah," I asked. "Why do you say that?"

"He used to give me a hundred dollars just to start his car."

It was all I could do to not laugh right in his face. If you haven't seen *Casino,* there's a scene where Ace's Cadillac blows up in the parking lot of a Tony Roma's restaurant. This part was dead-on accurate. Tony tried to kill Lefty with a car bomb. Lefty had an iron plate installed under the driver's seat, just in case. Lefty was a lot of things, but stupid wasn't one of them.

Lefty had this poor dumb bastard starting his car for him every day after work. Yeah. A real swell guy.

I had to ask. "Why do you think he did that?"

"Mr. Rosenthal said he liked to have the air conditioner running by the time he got in it. So he'd have me start it and get it going for him."

Lefty was probably worried they had poisoned the Freon, too, and this security guard was the canary in his coal mine. He was completely clueless as to Lefty's real motivations. I never told him, either. He probably sleeps better at night without that little piece of knowledge swimming around in his half-empty brain.

Once Lefty got tossed, Al Sachs was put in charge of the Stardust. Sachs was a real casino operator, but rumors were around that he was connected to the boys, too. Again, I'll let you put two and two together. This was right before I got there, so the things I witnessed were under Sach's watch.

In 1984, things came crashing down for the Stardust and their owners and operators.

It was a rare occurrence, but when the state Gaming Control Board simply had had enough of whatever bullshit these mob-run joints were doing, they pretty much threw them out. There was some legal wrangling, with due process and what have you, but once they went that route, whoever owned the joint was on their way out the door. When they did pull that trigger, Gaming put a trustee in charge, an already-licensed casino operator.

Whoever they put in that spot had a big leg up on purchasing the property. It was almost always on highly favorable terms. So getting that trusteeship was a big deal. What Gaming did with the Stardust was the biggest of these instances in Nevada history. They gave the trusteeship to the Boyd Group.

By then, I was the sports book director for the Cal Neva Casino in Reno. This is getting a little ahead of the chronology, but Warren Nelson, one of the primary owners and my biggest supporter, also owned a piece of the Boyd Group.

Boyd was a closed corporation, founded by Sam Boyd. Originally from Oklahoma, Sam, like hundreds of thousands of Midwesterners, had immigrated to Long Beach, California, where he ran a bingo game on a cruise ship before coming to Las Vegas. Once in Vegas, he worked his way up the ranks of the casino world. He bought a piece of the Sahara Hotel, then the Mint. He was one of the first operators to have a real marketing plan for contacting and retaining customers. By 1984, Sam had handed most of the operation over to his son, Bill Boyd. Bill was college educated and grew the company into a casino conglomerate that included the California Club and Sam's Town. Among the old-time casino operators, Sam and the Boyd Group had one of the cleanest reputations in the state.

I worked along with some of the Boyd Group people in the three years I'd been at Cal Neva. I had sat with some of them in meetings, exchanged ideas with them, and we even spent time in one another's casinos to see how other respected operators were doing business. When the Boyd Group was appointed trustee, Bill Boyd, Perry Whitt, Bobby Boughner, and Stan Weiss were all guys I'd known and had some dealings with. They were the ones charged with the day-to-day operations. They also knew I'd worked in the Stardust sports book a few years earlier. With that in mind, they asked me to come in, help them get the operation on the right track, and figure out how much the book was actually worth from an investment standpoint.

We went in the first day and a lot of guys who'd been in positions of any kind of authority were gone. If they hadn't left on their own, they were fired. The guys on the floor were just working stiffs doing what they were told by their bosses, who were now probably on the lam somewhere. The Boyd team went through the casino and count rooms, places in the Stardust I'd never been to before.

At one point, we were going through the slot procedures, walking the floor with a guy I remembered from my time there.

He opened up a machine and there were two buckets. Very casually, he said, "This one went to the count room and this one was for the money that was sent to Kansas City."

We all just kind of looked at one another in disbelief. He was telling us that this money stayed in the joint, to be counted, reported, and taxed, while this other money was the outfit's skim. Standard procedure. And everyone knew it.

Even though I've spent much of my life in the casino business, even becoming an owner, I don't really know a lot about casino operations outside the sports book. Helen Keller could have seen how blatant that two-bucket slot operation was, but scams from other areas of the casino were almost as blatant. Once we started going through the sports book, I knew what to look for in terms of how they were taking money out.

A lot of the records that should have been available were gone—for example, most of the winning tickets. All I could look at were the losers. I'm pretty sure a lot of incriminating evidence had been destroyed. It was no secret that Gaming was going to come down on these guys.

Some of the tickets I did see made me laugh out loud. I remembered one game where Michigan was a 3-point dog. The tickets were Michigan +12 for $2,000, Michigan +11½ for $2,000, Michigan +11 for $2,000, Michigan +10½ for $2,000, and Michigan +10 for $2,000. The rest of the tickets were Michigan +3. Unfortunately for the skim, Michigan got blown out in that game, which is why I was looking at all those losers.

In another game, they had the Phillies to win the National League Pennant at 100-1 for $1,000. If you bet $1,000 and the Phillies won, your ticket was worth $100,000. The ticket was written in mid-September 1982 when the Phillies had a big lead in the Eastern Division. Guess what? The Phillies blew the lead in the last couple days of the season and didn't even make the playoffs.

I tried to figure out how much of the business was legit

and how much wasn't. But there were so many phony tickets, I told them it would take me months to get to the bottom of it. I went through the past October with football and baseball in full swing and tried to make a reasonable assessment of what the basketball handle could look like. In the end, I told them I was really just taking a guess.

Nonetheless, I could see the sports book had a tremendous amount of potential. I said they pretty much had to just forget the past. The key would be to make sure they put the right management team in place and the sports book could be one of the best in Las Vegas.

On Warren Nelson's recommendation, they hired Scott Schettler to run the book. I'd replaced Scott at the Cal Neva, from which he'd departed amicably after a year or so running the sports book. He and I also had a pretty good relationship. When Scott was brought in, he really put the Stardust on the map as one of the industry leaders for the book and for himself personally.

Warren also wanted Scott to hire Roxy Roxborough to give him the line. Both guys wound up with stellar careers. Without the Stardust, they would have traveled much different paths.

Chapter 5

The Barbary Coast

In the summer of 1980, the Barbary Coast was expanding its operation. Jimmy Vaccaro, Sonny's brother whom I'd known since I was 12 years old, was the actual sports book manager. Uncle Jack was consulting for them, giving them the line every day and making the big directional decisions.

After my year at the Stardust I was offered a ticket writer's job at the Barbary Coast, but it held a lot more responsibility than I'd had at the Stardust. Uncle Jack and Jimmy had hesitated putting me in there a year earlier; I wasn't quite ready to have a position with any authority yet. But a year at the Stardust will prepare you for a lot of things in life.

Michael Gaughan was the primary owner of the Barbary Coast. Michael had a few partners, but Frank Toti and Kenny Epstein were most involved in the operation. Michael's father, Jackie, is truly one of the legends of Las Vegas. He was among the handful that made it a real gambling town and was as responsible as anyone for making the city what it is today. Jackie owned property and pieces of various casinos all over Las Vegas.

Michael himself now is among the legends for what he's done in the business, because he always understood how important sports betting is to marketing his entire casino. The way the sports book is viewed by the general public has a tremendous impact on the image of the casino. People talk about how liberal or tight a sports book is, because the odds are so visible and tangible. Even so, the sports book's bottom line is a blip on the radar compared to the pit, and almost nothing in relation to the slots, in most casinos.

Michael saw that the sports book brought in a lot of people. The Barbary became a regular stop for both wiseguys and the general public. One thing I learned at the Barbary (and I learned a *bunch* of things working there) was to offer a fair sports bet to everyone. To this day, so many places do all they can to run out the wiseguys by installing rules and posting lines that make it difficult to bet into. What winds up happening is they run out the regular players, the exact guys they *don't* want to run out. And guess what? The wiseguys still come in. Even if they can catch you napping for a couple hundred bucks, it's worth it to them. So the wiseguys keep coming and the public disappears. I've seen it my whole career.

With Michael and the Barbary, we ran a really good shop for everyone. Located on the corner of Flamingo and the Strip, we had Caesars, the MGM (now Bally's), and the Dunes across the street from us. Next to us was the Flamingo. Not a single one of those big-time casino-resorts knew how to run a sports book; they still don't to this day. All their big players started coming over to the Barbary Coast, which would take a bet. Caesars hosted big prize fights and I'm sure they did great business, but we had a ton of big play in our sports book. Once we got the high rollers, we didn't lose them either. Uncle Jack took a bet without flinching if he knew he had the best of it. Jimmy was in the same mold. Of course, you have to have the backing of management and with Michael and the other owners, we had that.

Uncle Jack didn't have an office. Instead, he ran everything out of the back booth of the Barbary Coast coffee shop. It became known as one of the most influential pieces of real estate in Las Vegas. Wiseguys and other big players knew to go to the back of the coffee shop to see what kind of prices and limits they could get. More action was written out of that booth than almost any Vegas sports book was doing at its counters. Uncle Jack knew how to maneuver in any type of business situation as well as anyone I've ever seen. Period. At another time and place, he could have been a general or managed a hedge fund or run a whole fucking country for that matter. I'll tell you this, not many in any walk of life would have gotten the best of him.

✎ ✎ ✎

Of course, Uncle Jack wasn't infallible.

In the summer of 1983, Michael Gaughan asked Uncle Jack if he'd like to take his family on a vacation to Michael's Vail condo. Transportation was no problem. Michael provided us the use of his private plane. In case you haven't picked up on it, Michael Gaughan is a hell of a guy.

One of the things we wanted to do while we were in Vail was go whitewater rafting. We found one of those touristy outfits that handled amateurs like us and made our arrangements. We got there nice and early and prepared to go on our all-day excursion on the wilds of the Arkansas River.

The guide gave us his speech about staying safe, the importance of remaining in the raft, and how to handle it if we fell out. He told us about the trip itself, how to paddle through trouble, what particular rapids were coming first, next, etc. Rapids were rated between 1 and 5, with 1 being a little ripple and 5 being like the Grand Canyon section of the Colorado River. We were going through mostly 1s, 2s and 3s. However, there was one 4 on our journey, where we had to be particularly careful. They called that section the Cannonball.

Just as we were taking our places on the raft, Uncle Jack turned around and stopped me. I could see he had panic in his eyes.

"Oh shit!" he said.

"What?"

"I forgot to leave my money back in the condo!"

"How much do you have on you?"

"About ten thousand."

Even today, it's far beyond me to question Uncle Jack, but at that age—I was only 27 at the time—it was out of the question. I also knew that Uncle Jack felt naked if he didn't have at least $5,000 on him. "Well, we're here," he concluded quickly. "I don't want to ruin the trip for everyone else. Let's go. I'll just try to hang on to it. Don't tell anyone about it."

We got in the raft, shoved off, and started our trip down the river. We were having a great time. The rapids were enough to get your heart beating a little, but nothing to really put the fear of God into you. Until, that is, we came up to Cannonball.

As we rounded the bend in the river, we could see far enough ahead that, yeah, Cannonball was pretty intense. The guide quickly went through his instructions again. "Most importantly," he yelled over the roaring river, "stay in the raft! This is not the place to try and swim through anything!"

Do I even have to tell you what happened next? We hit the rapids, the raft got tossed, and out went Uncle Jack in a full somersault. When his head bobbed up out of the water, I reached down and grabbed him by his shirt collar. As I was pulling him up into the raft, our faces were inches apart, I asked him, in a rather loud voice, "Where's the money?"

He quickly felt his pockets, "I've got it!"

I pulled him into the raft and we got through Cannonball with no further incidents.

But as soon as the water slowed, my cousin Nikki, the biggest drama queen in the family, by the way, started yelling at me. "I can't believe Uncle Jack fell into the water and you were worried about a little money!"

I looked at Uncle Jack, his eyes got wide, he gave a barely perceptible shake of the head, and said, "*Krypho*."

Krypho is Greek for, 'It's a secret.' But in this instance, a more nuanced translation would be, "Keep your fucking mouth shut."

At the end of the trip, Nikki started in on me again. "You were more worried about Uncle Jack's money than you were about him! I don't believe you!"

Of course I kept my mouth shut, enduring the wrath of Nikki, rather than disobeying a direct order from Uncle Jack. Two other cousins, Jack's two daughters Cindy and Olivia, started chiming in, too, giving me pretty much the same grief. I was defenseless, but what else could I do?

What they didn't realize was that if he said he didn't have the money, I was about to jump into the Arkansas myself and look for it. That would have been the stupidest thing I'd ever done, but at 27, I probably didn't have the judgment I have today. Still, I remember that I'd been ready to take that leap.

Even Zach pulled me aside and asked me what the fuck I was thinking. I couldn't keep it a secret from Zach and of all the people in the world I didn't want to think of me as a complete asshole, Zach was number one on the list. Once I told him, he started laughing. He knew there had to be more to the story. He also knew his dad would forget to take his money out of his pocket, even on a rafting trip. Meanwhile, for years, the girls didn't know the truth. It came up occasionally at family functions—"When Uncle Jack fell out of the raft, all Chrissy was worried about was where Uncle Jack had his money hidden." I do think back at how it must have seemed to them, with me grabbing Uncle Jack by the collar, holding him over the side of the raft, and screaming at him, "Where's the money?!" It had to look like some gangster movie with Jimmy Cagney or Humphrey Bogart threatening some sap with his life if he didn't spill the beans about where the dough was hidden.

About a decade later, after one of the girls told the story for the umpteenth time, Uncle Jack finally gave me permission to tell the truth about what happened. I'd borne the brunt of some pretty ill feelings till then, but they all got a pretty good laugh once they found out the truth.

At least they all knew I could keep a secret.

🖋 🖋 🖋

Uncle Jack was mostly a football and basketball bettor. Then one day ... He wanted to start dabbling in baseball when the season opened in 1981. His strategy was to "scalp" every game he could.

Scalping

A "scalp" is a riskless (arbitrage) play, most commonly executed in games lined close to pick 'em. It's most associated with baseball, but can be done in any game with a money line.

Here's an example. You bet the Dodgers +135 (risk $1,000 to win $1,350), while also betting their opponents the Cubs -124 (risk $1,301 to make $1,049). If the Dodgers win, you cash $1,350 and lose $1,301. If the Cubs win, you cash $1,049 and lose $1,000. You make a $49 profit regardless of the result.

These opportunities arise when a book is slow to move its number after the line has already changed in the marketplace.

Today, every sports book in the world has a screen telling them what everyone else's line is. Scalping games regularly is impossible now, but it was a lot more common before the Internet. I do see a lot of guys doing it today with props, or occasionally even some money lines.

Back in 1981, bookmakers opened their line, took bets,

and moved the number according to the action that came in. Amazing! And guess what? They made money! I wish today's bookmakers would do the same. Today, about 95% of the guys who call themselves "bookmakers" are really just "bet takers." They don't try to maneuver their prices off their action. They just follow the screen and if one of the big joints moves, they move. If the big joints hold a number, they hold a number. A monkey could run these sports books, because the suits who own and hire the managers would rather get mediocre results than pay someone who actually knows what he's doing. But I digress.

Uncle Jack had me going out in the morning, just after the books opened, and running around looking for numbers (I was working swing at the Barbary). Even back in those days, most books opened with close to the same numbers, so you had to wait a little while until they started getting some action to shake up the board. When I called him with the line, he told me what to play wherever I was. Then he scalped it on his end. We split anything we made.

There was no handicapping; we just went in needing every underdog. Most books took $2,000 or more, so if we did get a scalp, we had a chance to split $100. Some places took $5,000. If we got a scalp there, we had a chance to split $250. Not bad. Things were rolling along pretty well. I had one week where I made close to $2,000. That was a great time to be hustling for a living in Las Vegas.

In those days, the proper way to read the baseball line to someone over the phone was to say the name of the favored pitcher, then the price, then the name of the underdog pitcher. At the open, it was important to make sure everyone had the right starting pitchers. As the day wore on, you could then use the name of the team or the name of the starting pitcher when you ran someone the line. For example: If Steve Carlton of the Phillies was a -120 favorite going against John Candelaria of the Pirates, you would just say, "Carlton twenty Candelaria."

For Uncle Jack I skipped this whole routine. He told me just read the line; don't bother with the teams, pitchers, nothing. All sports books use the same rotation list for all the games, no matter what sport it is. A veteran like Uncle Jack followed along and knew exactly what the line meant as I read it to him. Uncle Jack isn't one to waste time. I read 'em, he told me what to play, and I was off to the next joint.

I started every day at Churchill Downs. This was a stand-alone sports book in a little strip mall where Paris Hotel Casino is today. Churchill took the biggest action in Las Vegas from the days when Bob Martin ran the place. Even though Bob had moved on, it was still one of the main spots everyone knew would take a bet. They really did have some balls. God, I miss joints like that.

We went through the ritual every day. By then, those guys knew who I was. I was giving them play on a couple games every day and of course my action was enough to move the number. They had no idea who I was moving for. They just knew me as some young kid who had a lot of money and bet some sharp numbers.

After finishing up at Churchill, I move on to the Santa Anita sports book, another standalone where the Venetian is today. After that I meandered my way through the various casinos and sports books in town, looking for numbers to scalp before heading to work at 4 p.m.

Then one day … I got to Churchill, like I always did. I wrote down the line, then ran it over the phone for Uncle Jack.

"Twenty, thirty-five, sixty, fifteen …"

About this time, I could hear him mumbling under his breath. "Jesus Christ … What the fuck?"

I kept reading. "Forty, eighty-five, a quarter, fifteen, pick 'em, seventy, forty-five, and a dime …"

"They have the Mets a dollar twenty?" he asked.

Beards and Movers

A "beard" or a "mover" is someone who's betting for someone else (usually a wiseguy). A beard is usually sent in specifically to hide the identity of the person making the bet, while a mover might be tied into a bigger betting operation, or syndicate, that employs workers to get their bets down.

I've never made it a point to throw out wiseguys, beards, or movers, but I like to know if a bet coming in is from a sharp guy or not. When it's a stranger, I have to guess if it's just a public bettor with a lot of money or someone betting for someone else who knows what he's doing.

That was the first game on the schedule. "Yeah."

"And the Phillies thirty-five?"

"Yeah."

"Holy shit," he said. Then he proceeded to read off all the bets for me to make. There were about 10.

"I'm going to run out of money," I said.

"Well, bet these." He mentioned the best ones. "Then come back and get more."

I bet the games he told me and ran over to the Barbary, which was less than a half-mile away. At Uncle Jack's booth in the coffee shop, I picked up more money, then went back and bet the rest. My next stop was Santa Anita. I read him their lines. They were similar, though with a few differences.

"I don't know what the hell is going on," he said, "but here, give them these plays ..." And he read me a list, almost the same as the plays at Churchill.

"How about the Tigers plus a dime?" I asked.

"No, that's the price everywhere."

"Churchill had the Tigers minus a dime."

"Are you serious? Why didn't you tell me?"

"Hey, it's my first stop. I don't know the favorites."

Remember, all I was doing was reading the prices, so there was no way for Uncle Jack to know that the favorite was flipped.

"You're right. Bet these, then run back over to Churchill and get the Royals even."

I did as I was told and went to the rest of my usual stops. There were a few off prices in some of them and completely crazy prices in others. It looked like some joints were getting this huge off-the-wall play and others were getting nothing, or maybe a few guys like me who were out scalping might move a number here or there.

The next day was almost a carbon copy of the day before. Churchill had prices that were totally different, as were Santa Anita's and the Royal Inn's, which was taking huge action at the time and had gotten some of this big play. The rest of the town looked like it had only been bet into by scalpers.

When I went back to the Barbary at 4 p.m. to work my shift, Uncle Jack pulled me aside. "I want you at Churchill tomorrow when they open. I want to figure out what the hell is going on. Tell me what you see."

"Okay."

The next morning, I got there when the doors opened at 7:30. I got a cup of coffee and started reading the *Daily Racing Form*. I kept a watch on the door to see if anything caught my eye, but for a long time, it was just a stream of the regulars.

Jolly Joe bounced in smiling, like he'd already had four cups of coffee. Montana Mel was writing down the line, so he could sing it to the guys he was servicing out of town. Hungry Hal, not a big bettor but a respected one, was swimming a river of shit and piss to get to the free donuts.

The other cast of usual characters like Nails, Blackie, Tips,

Mel, Ruby, Barney, Billy, Lem, Sam, the Captain, Injun Joe, Mustache Joe, Bobby the Midget, Bobby the Owl, Bobby the Beard, and Bobby the Tower all showed up. If this had been grade school, every one of them would have gotten a gold star for perfect attendance.

After about 45 minutes, I noticed a guy getting out of a Mercedes. He was about 35 or 40, a little chunky, with a dark well-trimmed beard. He had something in his hand that looked like a satchel. What really struck me was he was wearing these headphones with a wire attached that ran to a small plastic box-like thing clipped to his belt. And he wasn't just walking into Churchill. He looked like he was bebopping to the music as he sauntered into the joint. I had no idea at the time that I had just seen my first Sony Walkman.

Walkman Guy bebopped to the counter and I saw him nod at the boss, Gur. (Gur, Gurr, Grr, hell, I don't know. I just called him Gur. It's not like you had to pass a spelling test to bet there.) Walkman and Gur went into the back room for about 15 minutes. When they emerged, Walkman danced his way to his Mercedes and off he went. Gur went to the board and changed almost every number on the day's baseball lines.

I called Uncle Jack to tell him what I'd seen and give him the lines. He gave me the day's plays and told me he would take care of figuring out who this guy was. I'll steal a line from the movie *The Hundred Foot Journey*. In talking about the restaurant business, Madame Mallory says, "It's a secret society where everyone knows everyone else's secrets." That was the bookmaking business in Las Vegas when Uncle Jack occupied the back booth at the Barbary. By the end of the day, he knew all about the guy.

I was just a young punk ticket writer, so the next day Uncle Jack sent Jimmy Vaccaro to make contact with the guy. They got him to come to the Barbary Coast, where they said they'd put him on for the baseball under the following conditions: He could bet the first number for $2,000; they'd move the line a nickel. After that, he could bet $3,000 at the new number. Then they'd move it another nickel and he could bet as much as he wanted at the third number.

In baseball, or any bet that involves just a money line, when you move the game a nickel, it reduces the odds by 5¢. (No one used pennies in those days; everything was on the nickel.) If a bettor takes the underdog +125, then the line moves to +120 and he bets it again, the first bet wins $1.25 for every $1 bet, but the second bet wins only $1.20 for every dollar. A nickel difference. On the other side, if a bettor makes his first bet at -120, he puts up $1.20 to win a dollar. If it moves a nickel to -125, he has to put up $1.25 to win a dollar. Again, a nickel difference.

It turns out, I handled the first transaction. He came to the counter with Uncle Jack and Jimmy. There I was, pen in hand, at the ready. "Give me the Padres plus one-twenty-five for two thousand," he said.

I wrote the ticket. In those days, tickets were written on a triplicate form. One went to the customer, one went to accounting, and one was retained by the book for grading purposes (determining if it won or lost, and how much it paid if it won). They were hand-written. Of course, the money went in a drawer and was reconciled at the end of the shift. Today, the tickets are written on the computer. The customer gets the betting slip; grading and auditing are done by computer.

"Give me the Padres plus one-twenty for three thousand."

I wrote the ticket.

"Give me the Padres plus one-fifteen for a hundred and twenty thousand."

I looked at Uncle Jack and Jimmy. They both just kind of shrugged their shoulders. "We said he could bet as much as he wanted at the third number," Uncle Jack said. "Go ahead and write the ticket."

Mr. Walkman wound up playing anywhere from about $30,000 on up, with $120,000 bets his big plays, and he had a few of them every day. He was giving us about a million dollars in action every single day.

He turned out to be Hollywood writer/director/producer James Toback. Everyone in Las Vegas at the time knew all about it. We called him the Producer, even though he was more of a writer. The Producer just sounds more important. At that time, he'd written *The Gambler,* starring James Caan, which was what we knew him for. After that, he wrote *Bugsy,* starring Warren Beatty and Annette Bening, and *The Gambler,* a remake starring Mark Wahlberg. He also wrote and directed an interesting documentary on Mike Tyson. And he was a smart bettor who knew baseball as well as anyone I've ever met.

By moving the number like we did (I say we, though I didn't have much to do with it), it gave us a lot of leverage to take action the other way from more big players. After Toback made his bets, every wiseguy in town flocked to the Barbary to scalp the games, just as I'd been doing. All the smaller bettors made it a regular stop, too, because you never knew what kind of number you'd find.

🖋 🖋 🖋

My baseball scalping gig dried up. The Producer was now doing all of his betting at the Barbary Coast and I couldn't bet in my own book. It was worth it to me, because I had a lot of responsibility assisting in a book that took that kind of action. I was on the swing shift and even though I didn't have any fancy title, I had a lot of authority. If anything big came up, I never hesitated to call Uncle Jack or Jimmy, but they left me with the power to change numbers if I needed to and take action back on the side to put us in the positions we wanted to be in.

Usually, we tried to go in with the wiseguy sides and have the best of the number.

For example, if Toback had $100,000 on a game, we usually tried to get back about $85,000 the other way. If he had $30,000 (a small bet for him), we looked to get back $25,000. These were ideal situations, of course. Sometimes the bets that came in were more or less than what we wanted. It's just the nature of the business.

Taking a Position versus Balancing

You've probably heard that sports books "balance their action," meaning they take an equal amount of money on both sides of a contest to guarantee a profit. While that's solid in theory and is usually the goal, it's rarely the reality. There's almost always more money on one side than the other, either naturally or by design. When it's the latter, it's because the book has decided to "take a position" on a game based on what it thinks will happen. The book is still getting its -110 juice, but it's also gambling a bit. Some don't mind the extra exposure, whereas others prefer to play it straight.

My bookmaking philosophy has always been to take bets in the most advantageous way for the house to profit. I like to have some balance, but it's not my primary goal. If I have the wiseguys on one side and the public on the other, I'll do my best to go in needing the wiseguy's side to win (we wouldn't call them wiseguys if they weren't good). If I have a public bettor who I know isn't a wiseguy and is just straight-out gambling, I'll put him on for a big bet as long as he's betting what I believe to be "the right number," meaning he hasn't caught me in a mistake. Of course, this can lead to some very unbalanced games, but that's okay with me.

When Uncle Jack and Jimmy went home for the night, I was left with the chart of Toback's action. He had some parlays and round robins going too, so I had to keep track of those. Most of the time, no matter how much we needed to balance the books, they didn't want me to give away a price just to even out. They preferred to gamble with it. Michael and Frank were fine with it, so that's the way it was. Meanwhile, with Toback, the wiseguys betting back the other way, and our regular business, we were handling well over two million dollars every night out of a little corner sports book. What a great experience for a young kid like me who wanted to learn the ropes.

Kenny Epstein was usually on the swing and early grave shift. His father was an old bookmaker from Chicago and like all the other owners, he watched what was going on in the book every night. He had me calculate the average lay and take on each game. In the example of Toback's first ticket, he took an average of +115.28 on the Padres. If we could book action back the other way at anything above that, we were in good shape. He had me run every game like that. It was a great exercise for me and as simplistic as it might seem, it's a powerful lesson in common sense every bookmaker should be aware of.

My regular duties at the Barbary were writing, cashing, and grading tickets, moving the line, and balancing out the win/ loss figures every night for the book. Frankly, that's *way* too much authority to give to one person. Really, it was a license to steal, if I'd wanted to. In fact, shortly after I left the Barbary, Gaming tightened up the regulations to make sure sports book authorities and functions were more separated. It was just a matter of time.

Of course, the Gaughans had already been so great to me, personally, and the rest of my family, I wouldn't dream of stealing from them. And it was a smart decision on my part, because as good as they were to me then, it got nothing but better over the years. I'm glad to say I never did anything wrong. In all honesty,

I never even thought about it. Even though I'd seen so much larceny at the Stardust, I didn't want any part of it myself. Hell, if I had, I would have shaken Lenny's hand that day, grabbed an extra couple hundred, and just stayed at the Stardust.

I was really fortunate to have the opportunity to learn so much about the business while at the Barbary. First, working under Uncle Jack and Jimmy Vaccaro was an education that couldn't be bought anywhere. I also got to see successful casino people, like Michael Gaughan and Frank Toti, in action; both are still the top casino operators in Las Vegas.

Another great part was Jackie Gaughan, the patriarch. He loved to talk about the business. He came by and talked to me and plenty of other people. He didn't talk at us, but he actually discussed his ideas about bookmaking, told some stories, and asked what we thought, as well. One of my favorite people in the history of this business, Jackie's gone now, but having my path cross with his is another one of those lucky breaks I got in life. Jackie Gaughan is a real Hall of Famer.

I've done a few things in this business to brag about, but what I want to brag about most is this: I was very fortunate to make the acquaintance of the giants in the industry and I knew enough back then, and know enough now, to try to learn from each and every one of them. I see so many young guys on social media who think they have all the answers, guys in their twenties and thirties bragging how they buried the bookmaker or hit 70% in the NFL one year. After a while, they disappear, never to be heard from again. I had a wealth of knowledge come my way and I was smart enough to shut my mouth and listen.

I pass along a lot of that today and every so often I get some young kid, who knows everything, calling me Pops or Grandpa and telling me how out of touch I am. Well, there's a big difference between brains and wisdom, and the Pops and Grandpas of the world probably have a lot more wisdom than a kid with only a few years in the business. Do yourself a favor and don't assume you know everything. The smartest guys in this business tell me they're still learning new things all the time.

In an ever-changing constantly evolving landscape, it's wise to learn from guys who have been through it. If you're lucky enough, you'll be Pops or Grandpa someday. If not, that means you got killed along with every other two-bit gambler who thought he already had all the answers. And by the way, that's a huge favorite to happen to any gambler. If you refuse to listen to those who have gone before you, the price goes even higher.

🖋 🖋 🖋

Then one day … after a typical eight hours of Barbary Coast action, I had to balance the books. This involved the win or loss, as well as reconciling all the cash. I don't have an accounting degree, but I minored in accounting to go along with my business-management degree. It came in handy most nights at the Barbary, which was like my grad school.

This particular time, I tried balancing backward and forward for over two hours and no matter what I did, I was $250,000 short. That's not a misprint; I was a quarter of a million dollars short for one night. My shift ended at midnight and it was now two a.m. I'd been short before and I'd mispaid tickets, but this was outrageous. A quarter of a fucking million. I looked everywhere, I simply couldn't find it. Finally, I called Jimmy.

"Hello." I could tell I woke him from a sound sleep.

"Jimmy, it's Chris."

"Yeah?"

"Listen, I can't get this thing to balance." I swallowed hard. "I'm two hundred and fifty thousand short."

There was a pause on the other end of the line.

"Did you take it?"

He had to ask. We all have our price. Maybe $250,000 was mine.

"Well, no, I didn't take it. If I did, would I be calling you?" I'd have been on a plane to South America.

"All right. Turn it in. Auditing will find it in the morning." And he hung up.

Now, I know Jimmy as well as anyone. I guarantee he was back asleep in about 10 seconds. I wish I had a little more of him in me, too.

I still had to go to the cage to turn in the money I did have. The two cashiers looked at what I should've had and what I did have. Then they looked at each other. Then they looked back at me. I can only imagine what was going through their minds.

"Jimmy knows all about it," I said.

"He knows you're two hundred and fifty-thousand short?"

"Yeah."

"And what did he say?"

"He told me to turn it in. Auditing will find it in the morning."

They looked at each other again and shrugged. "Okay," they said without much conviction.

With that, I went home, went to bed, and had a pretty restless night.

This is one more striking example of how much the world has changed. Try turning in your cash a quarter-million short today. You aren't going home, you aren't passing Go, you're going straight to jail. Security, the cops, Gaming, someone is putting you in handcuffs. Fortunately, the Barbary was still enough of a family-run operation that that wasn't the case that night.

Like I said, I tossed and turned pretty good that night, until I got a call at about eight o'clock in the morning. It was Jimmy.

"They found it."

"What was it?"

"You had a hundred twenty-five-thousand-dollar ticket in the wrong column. You kept adding it. You were supposed to subtract it. Now get some sleep."

Last year, I was having lunch with Jimmy and Michael

Gaughan. Jimmy remembered the exact situation. We'd written the wrong team on one of Toback's tickets and we had to rewrite the ticket for him. Somehow, I got confused and once it got in my brain that way, there was no way for me to get it out.

Michael remembered it too. "I got in that morning and waiting on my desk was a note that the sports book was two-fifty kay short. If it was five or ten kay, I would have worried about it. But two hundred and fifty thousand, I knew it was just some stupid mistake."

We laughed about it at lunch. I guess we even laughed about it that day, once auditing found it. But I sure as hell wasn't laughing when I went home that night. Thank goodness it didn't happen with today's rules. Jail would've been easy. Hard would have been someone beating me with a bag of oranges in a back room to fess up to what I did with the cash.

✐ ✐ ✐

There was a baseball strike that season. So we had only a few months of booking Toback's action. He wound up beating us pretty good over that short period of time. Once the baseball strike hit, he was off doing something else. As far as I know, he never came back to town betting that kind of money again. He's had a pretty successful career in Hollywood and good for him. I always liked the guy. But man, I would sure like to get a crack at taking that kind of action again. That was truly a once-in-a-lifetime experience.

✐ ✐ ✐

There's a weird little story about my time at the Barbary that very few people know about.

As I mentioned, Jimmy Vaccaro let me move numbers if we were out of whack on a game. A few customers came in regularly

95

when I was on the graveyard shift to bet anywhere from a few hundred bucks to a dime. They asked me about small favors on certain games. If it looked like we were heading for a move or could otherwise use a bet at a good number, I let them have it for small amount, as long as we were getting other action from them as well.

Mitch and Sal, crap dealers from next door at the Flamingo, both about my age, were two of my regulars and we got kind of friendly. Mitch was short for Mitchell, though I have no idea if it was his first or last name. I don't remember Sal's real name at all. I just called him Sal, because he looked like John Cazale's character by that name from *Dog Day Afternoon*. Once in a while, I gave them an extra half-point on a game if we could use it. Besides, they were giving us a lot of square play, too.

Then one day … For some reason, they were desperate to get an extra half-point on a game we were running 3. If you're reading this and are a football bettor, I imagine you know how valuable any half-point on or off the 3 can be. If not, let me tell you: 3½ is much more valuable than 3. NFL football teams win by 3 points more than any other number. You don't just give away a half-point on or off that number. Mitch and Sal wanted to take +3½ and I just couldn't allow it. I had my job to do and we couldn't use any action at the number they were looking for. In fact, if we were going to move the pointspread at all, it would go the other way, to 2½.

They wouldn't let up. They ran over on their breaks to bet and each time, one or the other was back at the book begging me for that half-point. From the beginning, I told them they weren't getting that number. No uncertain terms. Period. Finally, they got the news that I wasn't going to yield.

In what I thought was an act of friendship, a no-hard-feelings kind of thing, Mitch and Sal walked in, having brought me a cup of coffee. Sal handed it to me. I thanked him and took a sip. That one sip let me know they spiked it with something. I put the coffee down while they were still there. Eventually, their break ended and they went back to work.

On their next break, Mitch returned and asked me, "How was that cup of coffee?"

Why on Earth would you ask a guy how his coffee was? It's not like he was a barista and brewed it or anything. We didn't even know what baristas were at that time.

"Great," I answered. "Perfect. Yeah, thanks a lot."

I saw them look at each other and then back to me. These two little pricks were trying to poison me over a half-point in a football game. They knew that I knew what they'd tried to pull.

I look back now and it was pretty stupid for me to keep this to myself, which I did. I wanted to get back at those two myself, extract some sort of revenge. Unfortunately, I never saw them again after that night. They probably had to skip town—and not because of me. Guys like that usually meet a bad end. Either that, or they become CEOs of multinational corporations. I know which outcome I'm rooting for.

✐ ✐ ✐

There's always that one guy who loses every bet in the most incredible, heartbreaking, punch-in-the-gut way possible. We had one of those at the Barbary Coast.

Stevie was the poker-room manager, a guy from back east who loved to gamble on anything and everything—poker, horses, craps, and of course, sports. If only he could win a bet once in a while. …

I was at the Barbary Coast nearly 40 years ago and anyone younger than around 55 might not realize this, but totals were pretty uncommon in most sports books at that time. Also, satellite and cable television were in their infancy. WGN out of Chicago and WTBS of Atlanta were the first superstations, local TV stations that went national via cable or satellite. In 1981, we picked up WGN out of Chicago on the satellite. It was like Adam and Eve eating from the Tree of Knowledge. A whole new world opened up to us.

Harry Caray was still with the White Sox and they or the Cubs were on every day. The Sox had a Cactus League game in Arizona one day and because it was on television, we put up a total (the Cactus League consists of teams that do their spring training in the U.S. Southwest). We did a ton of business, mostly because of the novelty of both the game being televised on a weekday afternoon and the fact that we had a total.

Stevie bet the game over 9 and by the fifth inning, each team had about 10 runs—a sure winner. However, baseball betting rules state that games have to go nine innings for there to be action on the total. A rain-shortened game negated the bet ("no action"). But it was typical Cactus League weather, with temperatures in the mid-eighties, sun shining bright, not a cloud in the sky. A rainout was the last thing on anyone's mind.

Stevie was whooping it up pretty good. He'd won his bet on the over early in the game and the money was as good as in his pocket. Both managers went deep into the bullpen in this game. I think there were about thirty runs scored altogether. No exaggeration.

But as the game wore on, the sun began to set behind the third-base line. Both managers were afraid that their first basemen could get hurt because of the blinding sunlight. They spoke to the umpires and the game was called after eight innings.

No action on the total. Stevie went nuts.

But you have to go by the rules, which are clearly stated. And if it sounds like bullshit, I can tell you that Gaming would greatly frown on a sports book paying a ticket that shouldn't be paid to the casino's poker boss. It would have skimming written all over it. Unfortunately, all Stevie got was his money back.

That's just a little precursor to let you know the kind of luck this guy had. It was all bad. And he wasn't quiet about it either.

He gave Cryin' Kenny a good run for his money. He ranted and raved, screamed and hollered with every heartbreaking half-point loss. And if a game ended with a miracle, you can rest assured it went against him.

Larry grew up in the same neighborhood as Stevie, though he was about 20 years older. He'd been in Las Vegas forever and when he learned that Stevie was running the poker room at the Barbary, he came on board. Larry was one of those tough old Jewish guys whose parents immigrated to this country in the early 1900s. Those guys grew up hard, with a certain ball-busting sense of humor that always cracked me up.

Larry came to my window and bet both sides of every NFL game for $22 apiece. When he told me what he wanted, I gave him this incredulous look, like, That's not what you really mean, right? Nope. He was adamant. That's exactly what he wanted.

I couldn't figure it out, so I asked one of the other ticket writers if he knew what it was all about. He told me that Larry had done the same to him the week before and he couldn't make heads or tails of it, either. Finally, we saw it.

Stevie came in Monday and carried on like always about losing this game or that in whatever incredible finish cost him his bet. And every time he did, Larry had a ticket on the winner. He pulled the ticket out of his wallet and held it up for Stevie to see. Stevie went immediately on tilt again, screaming at Larry for winning every goddamn bet when he needed the other side. This went on the whole season. Larry only bet with me and the one other guy and we never let on, even when Stevie came up to us and asked us what Larry had bet. All we said was he made us promise not to tell.

At the time, the NFL consisted of 28 teams, so that was 14 games every week. While Larry was guaranteed to have 14 winning tickets in his pocket, he also had 14 losing tickets. At $22 a pop, it was costing Larry $28 a week (betting $22 to win $20, he had to fade the $2 vig on each of his losing tickets for the 14 games) to keep the joke going, but to him it was worth it.

I left the Barbary Coast before the next football season came around, so I don't know how long it lasted. But watching Stevie go crazy every Monday during football was something I looked forward to every week.

Tilt

The term "going on tilt" is present in all of gambling. It's a reference to the old pinball machines that would tilt (lock up) when you pushed too hard on them. When a gambler tilts, he starts betting wildly in an effort to recoup losses, temporarily losing his sense of reason. In sports betting, it tends to take place when a guy goes off the rails after losing a bet he figured was a sure winner, also referred to as taking a "bad beat."

Chapter 6

On to the
Great White North

Scotty Schettler had been the sports book manager at the Club Cal Neva in Reno for about a year when he decided he didn't like being away from Las Vegas. Reno was certainly a much different town than Sin City. Plenty of sinning went on in Reno; the difference was Reno's brand of sinning would land you in the county lockup, where Las Vegas' sins would put you in Leavenworth. I'll leave the value judgments up to you. When I asked Scotty about Reno, he told me it was like the fading Monongahela Valley steel town of McKeesport with casinos. Western Pennsylvanians know that's not much of an endorsement.

I was offered the job to replace Scotty and wound up spending most of my career at the Cal Neva. After 30-plus years in Reno, I have to say I couldn't agree less with Scotty. I really like Reno and personally, I find that it offers a much better lifestyle than Las Vegas.

When I took the job, almost everyone told me I'd be back in Las Vegas as soon as I could find a similar position. Most Las Vegans don't realize Reno's climate is similar to theirs. A couple thousand feet higher in elevation and 450 miles north, it's usually about 10 to 15 degrees cooler. That's not too bad in the winter and a hell of a lot nicer in the summer. I have to remind my friends it's Reno, Nevada, not Reno, Alaska. I still hear from people who think it's covered in snow and we need chains on our tires all winter to get around. No. In fact, you can probably golf about 340 days a year in Reno. Try golfing in the middle of an August afternoon in Las Vegas and tell me how much you enjoy it.

Cal Neva is a great little casino on Virginia Street right in the heart of downtown. The ownership situation when I was there, however, was pretty strange. There were two primary groups of partners and, to put it nicely, they didn't get along very well. One group was chiefly represented by Leon Nightingale and Jack Douglass, the other by Warren Nelson. With their uneasy alliance, the two groups formed a sort of détente by allowing Warren to control the casino and Leon and Jack to control the rest of the operation, which included restaurants, entertainment, and maintenance of the facility. The sports book fell under Warren's jurisdiction.

Warren is not that well-known to many in Las Vegas, but he's truly legendary in Reno and among the old guard throughout Nevada. When they formed the Gaming Hall of Fame, Warren was one of the five original inductees. Among other things, Warren is considered the father of the game of keno in Nevada. Warren learned keno from Chinese immigrants working on the railroad in his native Montana and brought the game to Nevada. He was an original investor in IGT, the slot machine giant that dominated the industry for a time. Warren was also a good friend of Jackie Gaughan's.

Scotty gave plenty of notice that he wanted to go back to Las Vegas, so Warren had time to ask some of his friends in the industry for a replacement. He told people he was looking for a young guy who knew the business and would be forward-thinking and aggressive in running the book. Jackie told him about me and Michael confirmed that I'd done a good job for him.

Johnny Quinn was also a friend of both Jackie and Warren's,

and he too knew and recommended me. If you don't recognize that name, Johnny was originally from Omaha, like Jackie, and had built the Union Plaza Hotel in downtown Las Vegas. He was also the first to bring a computerized wagering system to the sports book industry.

Then one day … while I was still working at the Barbary Coast, Michael came by the sports book, gave me Warren's phone number, and told me to call him. He filled me in on what a great guy Warren was and how this would be a very good opportunity for me.

I called Warren later that day and after a brief conversation, he said, "Kid, I think I like you. Fly up to Reno tomorrow, so I can interview you for this job."

I made my arrangements and after a few hours of being interviewed by Warren, another Cal Neva partner Ad Tolan, and their general manager, Bill McHugh, I had the job about 24 hours after the first time I'd ever heard of the Cal Neva.

Things could get a bit contentious at times between Bill and me, but we wound up being good friends and worked together really well.

The one thing about Warren was the guy had some real balls when it came to taking a bet. I'm not exaggerating; he was as gutsy as anyone I ever met in this business and that's saying a lot.

He was a big tough bastard, a real Montana cowboy with a huge personality, somewhat of a blend of John Wayne and Ronald Reagan. He could be mean and crude as hell in one sentence and kind and heartwarming in the next. As our business grew, Warren always wanted to be the most aggressive sports book in Nevada. When I wanted to try something, Warren was almost universally behind it. God knows we had our beefs, like any boss-employee relationship, but overall he was fantastic and once again I was very fortunate to have him in my life. Chalk him up as another old-timer from whom I gained a whole host of knowledge.

ooo

Warren Nelson often proclaimed he was just a lucky guy. But it was more than that, much more. The Montana Warren grew up in before coming to Reno as a young man was, in a lot of ways, still the Wild West. The landscape was filled with carnies, tent-revivalist con men, real-estate scammers, and water-rights crooks. Warren learned his share from those guys and fit in perfectly with the lot of them. He also learned to deal all the casino games long before being on the legitimate side of the industry. And like all good gamblers of his day, he had a little larceny in his heart.

A lot of people can deal blackjack, but Warren had moves that would make Harry Houdini proud. He never showed me how he did it, but he challenged me to watch him and see if I could pick up it up.

"I'll deal you the ace of spades," he said.

I watched him shuffle, then cut the cards myself, and boom … there was the big black bullet. He could, in fact, deal me any card he called in advance. This came in handy at a blackjack game when, for example, a player doubled down on his 10 or 11 and the next card was a four. I'm a long way from being any kind of dealer, but I watched him shuffle and deal and never caught on. He was as good as any magician.

After opening its doors is 1962, the Cal Neva struggled, like most businesses do in their early days. By late 1962, Cal Neva didn't have the cash to meet payroll or pay its vendors. The casino was within days of closing its doors.

That was when Pappy Smith walked into the Cal Neva, sat down at a blackjack table, and bought in for $30,000.

Raymond I. "Pappy" Smith was an owner of one of Nevada's first casinos, Harold's Club. Harold Smith, Pappy's son, founded the casino, then took on his father as a partner. Pappy was more of a marketing genius than a gambling expert. Harold was the actual casino man, though Pappy was a great self-promoter who didn't hesitate to grab all the credit for himself, even trumping his son in the process. Though Pappy was quite flawed (he was married five times), he had a huge heart. He supported a few of his ex-wives through their late-life illnesses well beyond his legal obligations. And countless gambling losers got a rebate on some of their losses, just because Pappy felt sorry for them. You don't see too many like him in today's casino industry.

Even though Pappy Smith was no expert gambler, he wasn't likely to blow the entire $30,000 in a legitimate blackjack game. Yet, if he happened to win anywhere near the amount of his buy-in, Cal Neva was completely sunk.

Warren took the regular dealer off the game to deal to Pappy himself. Can you imagine a casino owner like Bill Boyd yanking a dealer off a game so he can deal to a high roller today?

No surprise, the cards quickly turned against Pappy. We'll never know what Pappy was thinking as he went through the buy-in, but we do know that he kept his mouth shut and kept on playing as he lost it all. When he was completely cleaned out, he stood, smiled, tipped his hat, and left.

Cal Neva made payroll, paid its vendors, and survived. Warren forever claimed that Pappy knew exactly what was going on. According to Warren, for whatever reason, Pappy must have figured that if he was being cheated so blatantly, there must have been a compelling reason for doing so.

A few months after Pappy's blackjack play, once his casino was out of the woods, Warren took $30,000 out of the Cal Neva cage, walked the one block to Harold's Club, and bought in to the blackjack game. A little while later, Warren had gone through his buy-in. He walked out of the casino and nodded to Harold Smith, who nodded back, then updated his father on the events of the evening. The debt had been repaid.

With Warren in charge of the casino, Cal Neva grew into a huge money maker. By the time he passed away in 2004 at the age of 91, Warren was a respected businessman, a veritable pillar of the community.

🖋 🖋 🖋

When I arrived at the Cal Neva, I didn't realize I was coming into any sort of political firestorm, but I was. The Cal Neva had recently expanded, doubling in size. Part of the expansion included a cabaret that brought in various acts. To call the acts B-list would be an insult to B-listers everywhere. It was struggling as an entertainment venue, to put it nicely.

Meanwhile, it was a great room with high ceilings and modeled like a classic Las Vegas showroom. It came with first-class dressing rooms, great lighting, and carpeted walls as was the style of the day, and it could seat about 300 people. Warren saw it as the perfect place to put a sports book. Even though Warren was almost 70 years old by then, he still had a great feel for how gaming was trending. He saw sports betting as the next big thing. Of course, he was right.

However, entertainment was in the Nightingale-Douglass territory. Converting the cabaret to a sports book was going to be controversial in the company, to say the least. Warren wound up getting his way, which was great for me, mostly. I was 25 years old and new to the company. But Messrs. Nightingale and Douglass saw me as allied with the enemy. I was under some pressure to perform.

Like any sports book, the win went up and down, but mostly up, fortunately. I could see Jack and Leon warming to me, but only a little. This was going to take some time. And where Warren could get away with doing whatever he wanted, I was still just an employee. I knew I'd need those two at some point, so I had to figure this thing out. Leon Nightingale was still chairman of the board and Jack Douglass was treasurer. They essentially controlled the purse strings of the company and they could be one tough sell when you wanted to make a serious investment.

For example, at the time, the NCAA put a host of restrictions on televising college football games. Only one, maybe two, games a week were being shown. They believed that excessively televising games would diminish their product. (Has the NCAA ever *not* had their heads up their asses?) The major football powers threatened to leave the NCAA and form the College Football Alliance, or CFA, allowing more games to be televised and earning more revenue as a result. They were bringing a lawsuit against the NCAA.

Satellite television was just emerging and the new alliance, were it to be formed, would use the new technology to show its games. Other sports were also looking into using satellites to show more games.

I saw this as a great opportunity for us to jump ahead of the competition by being the first sports book to get a satellite system. I talked to Warren about it and he was all for it. We then met with Jack Douglass. He wanted facts and figures before he would authorize the kind of money we needed to do this right. He ordered me to write a report for him.

I researched the hell out of it and presented it to Douglass a few weeks later. I had exhaustive notes on the chances of the CFA winning the lawsuit, the projected number of games that would be shown, how the other sports were now lining up to show more games on television, what it could do for our handle and win, etc. I had it printed, labeled, referenced, and footnoted like a college paper. Before then, I think Jack and Leon saw me as some street-kid bookie hustler. But based on the report, Douglass approved the purchase, we beat everyone else to market, and our handle and profits shot through the roof.

Not long after, in a quarterly management meeting, Leon singled me out for my performance in front of the rest of the team. Even though I'd started out on rocky ground, I'd now won over the other side. Not everything came up roses, of course; I had my beefs with some of the other owners and managers over the years. But by and large, they were all very supportive of me. When you're breaking new ground in business or any endeavor, it's important to have the backing of those who can pull the rug out from under you. Jack Douglass, Leon Nightingale, and later his son, Steven, all became big supporters of mine.

🖋 🖋 🖋

My son was born with some severe spinal defects. I don't want to go into too many details here, because that's not the tone of this book.

When he turned 18 months old in February 1986, my wife and I took him to San Francisco for surgery. I had two weeks' vacation coming and took them at that time to be with my son. The surgery wound up becoming much more complicated than we'd originally anticipated and my two weeks away turned into six. Since I had only the two weeks paid vacation, I had to eat the other four weeks I missed.

The sports book business was quite different in 1986. We got the line in the morning and after that, we just booked to our own business. There was no computer screen to see how the lines at other books were running or really anything else to help us along. Roxy Roxborough was servicing a few Nevada books by then, including ours, and he called with occasional updates if anything major was happening in the market.

Even though I was taking my vacation leave, I was calling every day to open the basketball. I was betting the hoops pretty good in those days, too, so I phoned in with updates and adjustments. There were no cell phones at the time, so I called the book collect. I already wasn't getting paid for my time and I sure didn't want to come out of pocket for the long-distance phone calls.

When I got back to work, Warren came to my office. He

asked about my son first, then about the collect calls. I explained everything to him, how I was still opening the line every morning, calling with updates, and generally handling all the business I could even though I had been away. He just kind of nodded, wished me the best with my son, and left.

The next day in my mailbox was a check for the four weeks' pay I'd missed out on by being with my son in San Francisco.

When someone mentions Warren Nelson to me, that's usually the first thought that comes to mind. He was one hell of a guy.

🖋 🖋 🖋

Warren and I grew very close and when the time came years later, Warren was a major advocate of my becoming a partner in the Cal Neva.

On the other hand, and to be totally forthcoming, many years later, Warren and I wound up on different sides of a lawsuit that became very personal between Warren and the rest of the ownership group. After a few days in court, their side dropped the suit. The whole thing was an unfortunate situation that tainted Warren late in his life.

A few years after the suit, right after I accepted a position at the Golden Nugget in Las Vegas, I called Warren to ask him if I could come to his ranch and see him. When I arrived, I found that he'd cleared everyone off his property, so we could spend time alone. I was there for about three hours and we rehashed a lot of the good and the bad times. We ended with a hug and a kiss, with both of us shedding a few tears. Warren was over 90 by then and we both knew it would be the last time we'd see each other.

It was something I felt I had to do, to get closure from a great man who was a tremendous influence on my career and me personally. I'm thankful I did that and very grateful to Warren for all that he did for me.

Chapter 7

Roxy

In my interview with the Cal Neva brass, I asked, "Do you want to bring in a lot of business or hold a high percentage?" In other words, do you want to offer fair bets that will attract a lot of action or tighten the screws on the bettors so we keep more of their money?

The answer: The primary objective was to bring in business. Of course, we didn't want to give anything away, but a high winning percentage wasn't what management was looking for. This was perfect for me. My philosophy then, as now, is to bring in the business and we'll make our money eventually. The whole Cal Neva casino operated this way, as did the restaurants with their 99¢ breakfast special, $2.99 prime rib dinner, and $1.50 hot dog and Heineken famous throughout northern Nevada and eastern California. And I was glad for it.

The Barbary Coast had a similar philosophy, but I could see I had to do some things a little differently now that I was in Reno. Scotty Schettler had been very aggressive in his bookmaking style. Even though he'd posted some bets I wasn't all that familiar with, I didn't want to lose any of the momentum he'd built.

If you remember, wagering on totals at that time was a brand new bet. Most places didn't offer bets on any totals in any sport. They were just getting a foothold in the marketplace. It was baseball season when I started at Cal Neva; basketball had just ended. I was getting the line every day from Uncle Jack, but I needed baseball totals. The Barbary Coast used them only on TV games, which were only the Cubs, White Sox, and Braves on cable and an occasional Dodger game on the local station. I asked him to get me totals on the other games, which he did. Unfortunately, they weren't very good. Every game was at -110 and most were on the whole number. You could forget about getting lines like "8.5 over -130" or "7 under -125." Even if they existed, most of the old-timers simply weren't into betting or booking totals. As a result, I opened with what Uncle Jack gave me and the few wiseguys hanging around were killing me on these baseball totals.

Then one day … I noticed Michael ("Roxy") Roxborough in particular was having a daily feast betting into my lousy totals. I knew Roxy when I was in Las Vegas, but not well. We just kind of nodded to each other when we crossed paths. I'd heard he was a pretty good guy, I just never had a chance to get to know him. But now he was in Reno for an extended stay, which I came to find out was a fairly regular affair for him. All he was doing was betting and while the market is much different in Reno than it is in Las Vegas, he could travel around and do well in northern Nevada.

As a bookmaker, I never had the attitude of treating wiseguys like the enemy. Probably because of my experience betting like a wiseguy (courtesy of Uncle Jack), I knew the best thing was to treat them right and try to go in with their side if you considered them sharp enough. While Roxy was betting at the Cal Neva, we started hanging out, having drinks and going to dinner almost every night. He had a lot of experience, mostly betting, but doing a little bookmaking as well. We spent hours discussing the business and different philosophies on how it all worked. As I've said before, one thing I'll brag about is how I've never been too proud or afraid to learn from others. Roxy had a lot of knowledge and I wanted to pick that brain of his.

Originally from Canada, Roxy started coming to Nevada to bet in the books just after turning 21. He had an analytical mathematical brain, which fit betting on sports and horses perfectly.

He's not afraid to talk to people either, so he got to know many of the main players in our business very quickly. You meet a few people along the way who love, I mean *love*, to talk about everything related to betting sports and Roxy was one of them.

He was one of the first to figure out "stadium effect" and how it influenced baseball totals. Every baseball stadium is different and those differences have a huge effect on how many runs will be scored in that particular ballpark. Before that, bookmakers just took into consideration the ERAs (earned-run averages) of the starting pitchers and maybe added a run or half a run, and that was it for formulating the line on a game. The lines weren't much different from the totals I was hanging on my board every day, then getting murdered.

However, when Roxy bet, and it was usually at least a couple bets at a nickel a whack, I asked him to let me know when he was finished. Once he was done, I asked him where he thought the number should be. He was done playing by then, so whether the line moved or not didn't matter to him. After he revealed his thinking, I moved the line to his number and kept taking action. His totals were way better than the ones I'd been getting from Vegas.

After a few weeks of him betting into me and going out together at least a few nights a week, Roxy told me he was heading back to Las Vegas.

"Why don't you call me every day with the totals?" I suggested. "And once we get to football, can you help me with the halftimes?" Uncle Jack wasn't doing much with the halftimes at that point. Without someone's help, I'd be on my own.

"Uh, sure," Roxy said. "What do you think it's worth?"

"I don't know," I said. "How about two hundred a week?"

"Yeah, okay," Roxy said, and that was the extent of our negotiations. We didn't sign anything, not even on a cocktail napkin.

He started calling me the next day and said, "You know, I might as well give you the whole line. Nothing wrong with having a different set of numbers to look at."

Eventually, Roxy became much more of a resource for me. While Uncle Jack was still the main guy for my game lines, Roxy was the nuts with totals. Being college-educated, he was highly mathematical in his approach. He was a few years older than I was, but we were both part of the new breed of bettor/bookmaker who wanted to offer more options in the sports book.

When Cal Neva got more aggressive with parlay cards, I created the first 10-point teaser card. Okay, I guess that's another brag, but yeah, I was the first. Roxy helped me with the math on the payouts after I'd charted a couple years' worth of results.

Years later, I invented the pleaser card and I ran that by Roxy as well before exposing it to the public.

I also started using Super Bowl-style propositions (usually, one-off bets unrelated to the final outcome of the game; props allow bettors to put their money on all manner of wagers, such as individual and team performances and the timing of specific events in a game) for every Monday Night football game. I was the first to do those every week, too. I was also the first to have a Monday Night prop card where ties *didn't* lose—in other words, a card that wasn't out-and-out robbery, very playable for the public and even wiseguys. I couldn't have done any of those without Roxy's help.

Obviously, Roxy was a huge influence on my career. Uncle Jack was unquestionably number one, but I would have to wheel Warren Nelson, Jimmy Vaccaro, and Michael Roxborough in the two hole to complete the exacta.

Once he launched his business, Las Vegas Sports Consultants, he was in northern Nevada a lot. Roxy, and LVSC, had a major impact on sports betting as it grew from shady operators in boiler rooms to the legitimate multinational industry it is

Two classic '70s' Las Vegas spots, both of which I frequented. Churchill was the wiseguy mecca. Tower of Pizza was owned by my Uncle Bobby Berent, one of Las Vegas' best handicappers and biggest players, and Jasper Speciale, the softest-hearted loanshark of all time.

My former boss and business partner Warren Nelson donated the money to build the football stadium at Carroll College in Helena, Montana.

Roxy Roxborough found this movie poster years ago and got it for me.

The Day the Bookies Wept was a 1939 comedy (of sorts) in which Betty Grable's character Ina figures out that Hiccup, the "race horse" her New York City cab driver boyfriend bought in Kentucky, can actually win with a bellyful of beer. She bets $2,000 at long odds, Hiccup wins, and bookies weep. I ran across the flick on Turner Classic Movies. It's awful, but I had to watch. Looking at Betty Grable eased the pain.

Roxy (right) and I back in the day

Family affair—
top to bottom:
With Uncle Jack,
Zach, Art, and
Pam

A sign from the famous Harolds Club, a Reno landmark. I found this in a sign graveyard in Kramer Junction, California. Pappy Smith became much more famous than the casino's founder, his son Harold. The chapter "On to the Great White North" contains a great story about Pappy Smith.

At the Tuscany Grill—*seated left to right:* Vic Salerno, Tony Sinisi, Walt Tendler, Johnny Avello, and Bob Scucci. *Standing left to right:* Nick Bogdanovich, Lou DeFilippis, Art Manteris, me, Roxy Roxborough.

Here I am, visiting the South Point before I was employed there. *left to right*: Bert Osborne (who preceded me as sports book director), Vinny Magliulo, Jimmy Vaccaro, and I.

Michael Gaughan loves to bust Jimmy's balls about getting more publicity than the owner. While the VSiN studio was going up in secret behind this wall, Michael put up this sign, in part to get people wondering if Jimmy actually built the place and in part to do one more thing to get Jimmy's goat.

Clockwise from the top: me, David Purdum, Roxy Roxborough, Anthony Curtis, Hank Goldberg, Chuck Esposito, Naj (Sunset Station marketing director), Art Manteris, and Vic Salerno.

The girls of the South Point sports book dressed for Halloween 2016. *left to right*: Kam, Khristine, Gosia, Aracely, Eva, and Shelly.

In the studio: I'm surrounded by Vinny (left) and Gill Alexander

From left: Brent Musberger, Vinny Magliulo, myself, and South Point casino host Dave Jensen at the Knights-Blackhawks game. It was the first time my doctor gave me permission to go out after being sick for months.

Upon the official opening of VSiN, Brent Musburger came in on
the Budweiser wagon. *left to right*: Ryan Growney, Vinny Magliulo,
Michael Gaughan, Brent, me, and Jimmy Vaccaro.

Above: In the VSiN studio, Brent to
my left and to my right comedian
Norm MacDonald, who was ap-
pearing at the South Point.

Vinny Magliulo, me, and Jimmy
Vaccaro grace the cover of VSiN's
Point Spread Weekly.

Brent with my daughter Jacque. Brent was happy to learn Jacque is now a resident of Montana, Brent's home state.

Uncle Jack and I dressed for Rodeo Days at the South Point. This is not how we dressed in Pittsburgh.

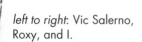

left to right: Vic Salerno, Roxy, and I.

today. All that from supplying me with baseball totals for $200 a week. Yes, you can say he was lucky to run into me, but I was lucky too. I don't think I would have had nearly the success in my career if it weren't for Roxy.

Besides that, he was a great friend. I couldn't begin to guess how many times we went to dinner, drove up to Tahoe, went to a track to play horses, or wound up drunk and thrown out of Greek restaurants together. (Okay, that was only once, I swear.) I've always had a great time with the guy no matter what we did.

I could always say I knew him when … he was building his business and sleeping on my couch. And what a business he built for himself. At one time he serviced the majority of sports books in Nevada. He's been recognized for years as one of the authorities in the industry. And to think, it all started with him kicking my ass betting baseball totals.

Chapter 8

Max

When I look back at my first days at the Cal Neva, it hurts me to say, but I was probably a bit of a mark.

I was new in town, making good money, only 25 years old, and didn't know a soul. A few people are always looking to jump on someone vulnerable, like I was, and they often do. Little did I know that one of them would be Meyer Lansky's hitman.

Lansky is probably the most famous Jewish mobster of yesteryear. He had associations with some of the Italian mobsters of his time, but many of his closest confidants were Jewish. Enter Max Kurschner.

Max was a good horseplayer in the race book at the Cal Neva. I tried to get friendly with any and all of my good players at the time and he was one of my best. After a few weeks of nothing more than the same casual relationship I had with a few of the good players, Max started inviting me to have coffee or a drink with him after work. It soon evolved into dinner.

One night after a few drinks, Max told me about what he did for a living—"taking care of" Meyer Lansky's enemies. And when he said "take care of," he didn't mean attend to or caregive or nurse them. In fact, it was the exact opposite.

This was a pretty bizarre admission and I wasn't sure what to make of it. He found out a little about my background and knew some of the same people I did, so there was definitely something there, but I just wasn't sure.

Then, soon after admitting this to me, he told the same thing to a few other people in Reno, in particular at the Cal Neva. Some people believed him and some people didn't.

I knew an older guy who had been a bookmaker under Lansky's protection. I managed to reach out to him and asked about Max. He told me he didn't know him and certainly didn't recognize the name, but he sounded like the kind of guy who'd do Lansky's dirty work. I'll never forget his last words to me before we ended the phone call: "Be careful." Why? Because Lansky and his outfit had a reputation of being extremely violent.

I'd begun dating a girl who was working for me, Sharon. This wasn't exactly kosher and it was something we kept secret. I was in love with her and she eventually became my first wife, but at the time we had to keep it under our hats.

In the meantime, Max was also very interested in Sharon. He was practically drooling over her every day in the race book. I couldn't blame him; she was a beautiful girl. She kept rejecting him, without really giving him a reason. Max even asked her to marry him, though she had the brains to turn him down.

Eventually, I went to my bosses and told them about Sharon and me. We were getting pretty serious and I wanted them to hear it from me rather than find out on their own. Max found out at the same time and claimed there were no hard feelings; he was glad she was with a nice guy like me. I believed he meant it, but you never know what's in the heart of someone who's in love, or at least infatuated, and has been rejected.

Things went on for a few months without any incidents worth noting. Max bet his horses and won and lost like everyone else. We went to dinner and had a few drinks now and then. I tried to keep my distance as much as possible, but it seemed I'd opened a door that was very difficult to close. Also, I could see his action was getting smaller and smaller over this time, so I had a feeling he might be running out of money.

One night when we were out, he asked to borrow $800. He

said he had a package coming in any day now, but needed cash to hold him over. I might have been a little green, but I knew anytime someone tells you about "a package coming in," you can be assured it's bullshit. I wasn't exactly flush with cash at the time, but the $800 wouldn't kill me, either. Besides, I figured if he was going to stiff me, it might be an easy way to get him out of my life. So I gave him the $800. A few days later he disappeared. I wasn't that surprised or sorry. If the money got rid of him, it was well worth it.

A couple months later, Sharon and I had a day off and took a ride to Bay Meadows, the racetrack just outside of San Francisco. We went into the turf club, got a table, ordered some food, and made a couple bets. Between races, we went to the bar. While we standing there, who came around the corner but Max?

I don't want to pretend I was all that worldly and knew how to handle mob guys, but as I mentioned in the "Stardust Memories" chapter, I did know a thing or two. First, you didn't want to let them push you around, but offending them wasn't the smartest thing in the world, either. You're living on a knife edge and you don't want to slip.

"Hey Max," I said, then turned to Sharon and said, "Go take a walk." If he was going to kill me, the last thing I needed was for him to kill the one person who could identify him, and whom I also happened to be in love with. I can still see the surprised look in her eyes as she turned to walk away. She knew this could be serious. And it was; I was afraid Max might kill me mostly because he was a complete loose cannon with a terrible temper, he owed me money, and I was dating his sweetheart—plenty of reasons to be afraid he might do something rash.

My heart was pounding out of my chest. I was definitely scared. I wasn't sure what was going to happen.

We exchanged pleasantries for a few moments, then I had to ask, "Max, am I ever going to get my eight hundred back?"

"I couldn't come up to Reno."

"Why not?"

"I was in the hospital for a month."

"You were in the hospital? With what?" He looked pretty healthy to me.

"I got shot!"

One thing about Max, he was kind of little, though he was pretty thick with muscle. He was also the kind of guy who was constantly gaining weight, then going on some crash diet and losing it, then inevitably gaining it all back. I'd never seen anyone who could have such a different physique from one week to the next. When I ran into him at Bay Meadows, he had definitely put on quite a few pounds from the last time I saw him.

"Well," I said, "congratulations."

"What do you mean?"

"You're the first guy in history to go into the hospital for a month and put on thirty pounds."

He started laughing and when he did, I was pretty sure he wasn't going to attack me. But I've got to say, my heart was still on overdrive. If he did kill me right then and there, my ghost wouldn't have been floating around saying, "Geez, I never saw that coming." I was definitely afraid it could be coming. Nonetheless, I felt had to say something, even as smartass as it was, just to let him know I knew he was handing me a crock of shit.

"I know, kid, I know," he said. "You were good to me. I'll come up soon and make things right between us."

"Okay, Max," I said and shook his hand. I have to say, I was pretty relieved it ended like that. Like I said, I didn't need the $800 all that bad.

Back in those days, we didn't have the Internet or Twitter or anything like that, so if you wanted to stay informed about the goings on in the sports world, you got the out-of-town newspapers. The *San Francisco Chronicle* was one of the best and I made sure to get it every day. One day, on the front page of the local section, it had the story of a man who'd been gunned down in the parking lot of a motel in San Mateo, a town in the south Bay Area. It was Max.

It just so happened, right next to the story was picture of Meyer Lansky, who'd been indicted or something. There was no reference in either article about the relationship between the two of them. Someone on the copy desk, though, had to know something. It couldn't have been a coincidence.

Subsequent stories did make mention of the possible connection between the two. One also mentioned that on Max's tax return one year, he put as his profession, "salesman and hitman." Also, a book co-written by David Fisher, *Joey the Hitman: The Autobiography of a Mafia Killer*, was about Max. He used the pseudonym Joey Black, but people knew it was really Max. He claimed to have killed 53 people in his career.

Max's killer was never found, or at least never arrested and brought to trial. Even though Max spent a lot of time at the Cal Neva, I never once heard from the police. You'd think they would at least ask a few questions. Heck, I'm surprised I wasn't a suspect or at least a person of interest.

All this time has gone by and I still don't know exactly what to think. A mystery surrounded Max, just like it does Lansky. Some people claim Lansky died broke and there's some evidence to support that. Other evidence indicates he had more than $30 million in secret bank accounts. Even the most qualified experts aren't sure.

The same can be said about Max. I'm not sure how much was true and how much was pure bullshit. But I do know he was gunned down in a motel parking lot and that doesn't happen to just anyone. Something nefarious was going on.

Fortunately for me, he had only killed 53 people. If it had been 54, I might not be here.

My heart still starts racing every time I think of this story. I got awfully lucky.

Chapter 9

Adventures in Bad Bookmaking

In any new industry, there's always a shakeout period. Lots of hopeful, wannabe, and delusional people jump into the business during the early wildcat years, many of whom aren't qualified, are totally incompetent, or are complete idiots.

For a long time, Nevada sports books couldn't be housed within a casino. I'm not sure about the logic behind this regulation; nonetheless, it was there. Sports books were small standalone places like Churchill Downs and Little Caesars.

Once the regulation was revised in 1974, the Union Plaza was the first to put a sports book in a casino. The Stardust followed soon afterward. When other operators saw how sports books enhanced these two properties, most of the major players wanted to add one. Some viewed it as a profit center. Others considered it simply as an amenity to keep their customers from leaving the building.

Regardless, suddenly, numerous new jobs became available. Some were filled by guys who knew what they were doing, but a lot were occupied by—well, let's politely say—guys who didn't. Either way, with the tremendous expansion in the industry, there was a lot of opportunity and if you knew what you were doing and kept your nose clean, you could make a career for yourself.

This sudden burst of bookmaking gave me my chance at

Cal Neva. It also put some guys behind the counter who had no business being there.

It's a syndrome you see in many businesses: The higher-ups feel that any job below their level has to be easy. And after all, sports is something almost everyone knows at least a little something about, plus most guys applying for a job in a sports book have probably made a bet or two in their lives. Naturally, the geniuses in the boardroom think anyone can be a bookmaker. What is there to it? You get the line, put it up, and players hand you their money. They look around at the mid-level managers and pick a guy who looks good and reads the sports page every day, and voila, here's our new sports book manager. The way the industry is today, casinos can, and do, get away with it. Today's sports book managers are bet-takers, not bookmakers, and though the results are totally mediocre, it's the way of the corporate business world.

Once the Cal Neva sports book really began to take hold, it first caught the eye of the Comstock Hotel in Reno. There was some cross ownership between the Comstock and the Neva, so the temptation was there to copy what we were doing down the street. The Comstock executives were convinced they could duplicate it. If only it were that simple.

Comstock management and the partners who weren't involved in the Cal Neva were greatly jealous of what we were doing. They had a nicer facility only three blocks away. It always bothered them that it was so hard to be as successful as we were. They promoted a keno manager, a nice guy and a sports fan, which made him qualified, right?

Because of the cross ownership, I helped the guy, Louis, get started. Eventually, I told him I couldn't run his book and mine at the same time. He had to step out on his own. Roxy Roxborough was getting his Las Vegas Sports Consultant business off the ground, so I told Louis to call Roxy. It was a true win-win: Louis got the best info in the business from Roxy and all these incompetents new to sports betting helped Roxy's company take off.

Roxy gave Louis the line in the morning, like he did to all his customers, and with the Cal Neva connection, I think he tried to take care of him. Louis kind of knew how well the Neva was doing with parlay cards and he wanted to do the same. Of course, he knew nothing about them, so Roxy had to walk him through the whole procedure, including how to make a teaser card off the parlay prices, either by adding six points to the underdog or subtracting six points from the favorite.

Then one day ... football season was winding down. It was that funky period between the last college game and the bowl games. Another thing youngsters might not realize is that only about 15 bowl games were played back then. Louis wanted more action for his parlay card, so Roxy gave him a handful of basketball and hockey games. Now, also remember, hockey games could end with the score tied back then. So when two relatively equal teams were playing, the home team was usually favored by a half-goal.

Roxy called all his customers throughout the week. When he called Louis on Friday to check in on how the business was going, Louis exclaimed, "These teaser cards are the greatest thing ever!"

As soon as Roxy heard that, he knew something had to be wrong. The teaser cards weren't the best thing ever and never will be. "What do you mean?"

"I'm getting a ton of action on them," Louis said.

"Who are they betting?"

"That's the best part. I'm getting great two-way action."

"Well, tell me which sides they're playing."

"I have X amount (I'm not sure how much exactly) on the Canadiens +6.5 and about the same on the Bruins +5.5."

"You used hockey on the teaser card?"

"Oh, yeah. I've got a ton of action on all the games."

"You can't use hockey on a teaser card!" Roxy said. "They're only for football! You have to scratch those games. You're going to lose every one."

"You never told me!" Louis said.

Naturally, Roxy never imagined a guy running a sports book, a legal bookmaker in the state of Nevada, could possibly be so clueless. How wrong he was. If you're not a hockey fan, adding six goals to either side of a hockey bet would create such an outrageous advantage that it would be hard even to calculate. Only about one game in more than 100 would be decided by six goals or more.

"Just scratch the games. Don't take any more bets on them. You have to tell your bosses right away."

Of course, they lost every game and within a few weeks, the Comstock sports book was gone. Closed. Never to be heard from again. The whole Comstock wasn't far behind in shutting its doors entirely.

Years later after I'd become a partner in the casino, my first wife and I divorced. The Cal Neva was coming off two consecutive record-setting years. The judge drew a trajectory of those two years like the gravy train would never end for the Cal Neva. We didn't have rooms, but he even allowed my wife's attorney to introduce conjectures that we would eventually have rooms and my stock would essentially double in value.

Needless to say, we never came close to having years like that again. We never did build rooms, though we bought the Virginian, the (piece-of-shit) hotel next door. In fact, the stock value went on a slow decline for a variety of reasons. Still, the judge really stuck it to me.

Only after I'd signed off on everything did someone inform me that the judge had owned a piece of the Comstock, which by then had long been closed. My lawyer advised me not to do anything about it. The next judge would probably stick up for the first one.

Once I found out, I could see the judge was totally biased as to how much money I would eventually make from Cal Neva. Let me be clear, I made a lot, but it was nowhere near what the guy in the black robe thought it was going to be. And when I did finally sell my stock, I got back exactly what I paid for it, not a penny more. In all honesty, it wasn't even worth that; it was just that my contract stipulated they had to reimburse me at least that amount. So thanks to that judge and his jealousy of Cal Neva, he cost me hundreds of thousands of dollars. Fucking Comstock.

✍ ✍ ✍

In the late 1980s, Scott Schettler, whom I replaced at Cal Neva, was running the sports book at the Stardust. Scott, along with Roxy's help, wanted to provide the opening line each week for football. Of course, this was at least a decade before any offshore books or the Internet. The other sports books around Nevada were content to let Scott and the Stardust open, take action, and get the line hammered out before the rest of us put up the lines on Monday. It was a wild scene every Sunday night at the Stardust, which had to go through a few iterations of the betting rules. Bettors were standing in line for hours. One of the famous handicappers was Dick the Picker, who spent years in the state of Washington picking apples, until he built up a big enough bankroll to bet full-time. Dick got in line first and bet the whole board before anyone else had a chance. Then the guy behind him bet into what was essentially Dick the Picker's line. Then the next guy would bet, and so on.

There were fights to get in line and at least once, a guy pulled a gun just to get a spot. Stop and think about that. A guy pulled a gun so he could give the sports book his money. I don't know about you, but if I pulled a gun, I'd probably be looking to *take* someone's money, not hand it over to someone.

Soon, Scotty changed the rules where you could bet only three games, then had to go to the back of the line. This worked for a while, but there were still fights to get in line and Dick paid guys to stand in line for him. Eventually, Scotty instituted a lottery. You had to come in and sign up, then the names were pulled out of a drum for the betting order. You could bet only one game at a time, then you had to go to the end of the line and wait your turn again. It was nuts.

Meanwhile, the word was getting out that the opening line was pretty accurate after all. I'm not sure what kind of profit, if any, the Stardust made on their openers, but it wasn't highway robbery, like some handicappers had you believe. No, the games won and lost like anywhere else and the Stardust wound up doing okay, at least with all the subsequent action they booked during the week. In the end, opening first was great for their business.

✐ ✐ ✐

Many times, I've seen upper management waiver between being scared to death of wiseguys and maintaining that the opening line is just this side of absolute science. Indeed, they switch back and forth from week to week, depending on how their book did or how they themselves did with their own personal bets. They think they understand the business, but have no idea what real bookmaking is. Actually, a good opening line is valuable, but you have to manage and massage it along the way. It's not terrible and it's not perfect. Sports betting is neither the most nor least efficient market in the world.

Not many people knew this, but I was making personal bets at a sports book in Reno where the managers believed the opening line was near perfection. Lord knows I wasn't going to tell anyone about it. The sports book manager, "Bill," was one of those typical poor hires, a management guy in some other capacity who read the sports pages and made an occasional bet. He was a big good-looking guy. Honestly, he could have been a model. He had the perfect hair and build and he happened to be a really nice guy.

Bill posted the Stardust's Sunday-night opening line at 11 a.m. Monday. After the games got bet and the lines got massaged and manipulated, some games moved like crazy, some hardly at all. Nonetheless, Bill put up Sunday's line, no matter what it was. By then, of course, *I'd seen all the moves*!

The biggest advantage a bettor has is he doesn't have to make a bet. I had the luxury of betting all the games that moved, but only if I liked them. For example, Purdue might open -6, and if the line moved to -7, I could still get it at -6. If I didn't like the move, I passed. I usually gave Bill anywhere from 10 to 20 plays every week, often hitting a game a couple times. Where I wanted to play against the move, I just bet the games somewhere else. I was always almost 100% done with my college betting for the week by one o'clock Monday afternoon.

God only knows what percentage I won, but let's just say it was pretty goddamn good. Only one other guy knew about this and I don't think either one of us ever told a soul. If Dick the Picker ever found out, our little slice of heaven was finished. This lasted about two football seasons, until the upstairs brass figured out they had to make a change. When they put the new guy in, it was a sharp bookmaker who actually knew what he was doing. My gravy train had been derailed.

I have one more example of what Bill would let us do. I don't know if it was worse than the football line, but it's close. I'll let you decide.

On the big fights, and there were a lot more of them in those days, Bill put up multiple "will go/won't go" prices (over/unders on rounds). A fight might have "will go 7 rounds -140/+120" and "will go 9 rounds +130/-150." Don't quote me on those prices; I was never much of a fight guy. But I think you get the idea. For those who don't, they mean the fight is a favorite to go the seven rounds, given the bet of $140 to win $100, as opposed to the underdog bet of $100 to win $120. Same with nine rounds: bet $100 to win $130 that it goes nine or bet $150 to win $100 that it doesn't.

If I liked the go/won't go (usually from someone telling me that I should), Bill would let me parlay one price to the other. In other words, if I liked the fight to go nine rounds, I could parlay "will go 7 rounds -140" to "will go 9 rounds +130." Let me explain. If the fight does go nine rounds, it has already gone past seven rounds. If you parlay the two, you're getting paid the rate for a 2-team parlay, rather than a straight bet. If you bet the "won't go 7 +120" and "won't go 9 -150," it worked the same way. If the fight didn't go seven rounds, well, of course it didn't go nine rounds either.

At least one other guy, a friend of mine, bet these parlays. We kept our bets small, no more than $200 a pop. It was a great little pick-up for us. Sometimes we bet both sides and just split it. I don't think we ever got middled, not once. Then one day … we bet it, Bill looked at the ticket, and said, "Geez, if it goes nine rounds, I guess it's already gone seven."

My buddy and I looked at each other and played dumb. "Oh, yeah. Never thought of that."

Bill took away our parlay privileges after that. But by then, it didn't matter. He was gone soon after.

✑ ✑ ✑

Before Roxy got started in his legitimate business in Nevada, he'd been servicing a couple guys around the country by giving them betting lines. I knock the corporate bookmakers plenty, but believe me, plenty of incompetents ran local books, too. One of Roxy's favorite stories is about a local who maybe wasn't the sharpest bookmaker around.

As I've mentioned, totals were a new bet in the mid-1970s, posted for football only. Even into the late 1970s, college basketball totals were unheard of, except in the major games, the one or two we could get on TV on Saturday or Sunday afternoons. That was it.

While most conferences spread their basketball games throughout the week, the Ivy League plays its games on Friday nights and Saturdays. The travel is usually easier and, of course, the Ivy League being about students first, Fridays and Saturdays were less stressful academically for the players.

On one NBA All-Star weekend, the four Ivy League matchups were all the basketball action there was for that Friday.

"Can you get me some totals for these Ivy League games?" the bookmaker asked Roxy.

"I don't see any posted. I'd have to make them myself," Roxy said. "They probably wouldn't be any good. Why do you need them?"

"If I don't at least have some totals, there won't be enough to bet on. I won't do any business today.'

"I hate to give you something that I don't think will be any good."

"If I lose, I promise I won't bitch about them. C'mon. Just give me a little something for my customers to use in parlays."

"Okay, okay," Roxy finally conceded. "Give me about an hour and I'll make some for you."

Now remember, these were the days before the shot clock. In the '70s, it wasn't exactly peach baskets and white guys shooting set shots, but the Ivy League was a far cry from today's basketball product.

Roxy called the guy after an hour or so. "Okay, here you go. Cornell and Dartmouth ninety-one, Penn and Princeton ninety-eight and a half, Columbia and Brown eighty-nine, and Harvard and Yale ninety-two and a half."

"Okay, Roxy. Geez, thanks a lot."

"Now, don't take too much on these. I don't have much faith in them."

"I won't. Thanks again."

Roxy didn't think much more about it until later that afternoon. About a half-hour from tip off, Roxy called the guy.

"How's the action?" Roxy asked.

"These are the greatest thing ever!"

As I've indicated before, nothing is the greatest thing ever. And college basketball totals have never been and never will be the greatest thing ever for a bookmaker. Roxy knew right away something was wrong. "What do you mean?"

"I'm doing so much business on these things, you can't believe it."

"Well, tell me what the plays are."

"Okay, the Cornell game, I opened one-ninety-one and I'm all the way down to one sixty-five— "

"I didn't say one ninety-one! I said ninety-one! Don't tell me you did that with all the games!"

"I was wondering why all the action is on every under."

"Jesus! You're going to get annihilated. You'll lose every game. See if you can settle with some of these guys before tipoff."

He might have made some arrangements with some of the guys, but with the rest, annihilated he was. And soon out of business.

✎ ✎ ✎

When Roxy was in Reno, we usually took a day and headed up to Lake Tahoe to play the horses, drink, chase women, and have dinner on the way home, then do it all again the next day. Of course, we were both running our businesses, so we couldn't take off every day, but it sure seemed like we did it a hell of a lot.

Sometimes the hangovers were too bad and we didn't make it to Tahoe in time for the first post at Belmont, Saratoga, or Aqueduct. On those days, we stumbled into Artichoke Joe's, the lone race and sports book between Reno and the Lake.

Artichoke was one of those bookmakers who hated wise-guys. *Hated.* He got so tired of losing in NBA totals, he devised the "coconut line." Why was it called the coconut line? Because "you had to have your head full of coconuts to bet into it!" Or so said Artichoke.

Artichoke would use a 4-point spread on the totals. If the total was 210, Artichoke's over was 212 and the under 208. You still had to lay -110 either way. So every game he had a 4-point middle working for himself. And he never moved the line. He figured the 4-point middle with juice his way was all he needed.

In those days, some sharp handicappers were betting NBA totals that moved 7 or 8 points on a regular basis. When Roxy and I had to make our occasional stop at Artichoke's to get down on the first at New York, we wrote down the basketball lines. If it was worth it, we cut our day at the Lake short and hustled back to get down on a total that we knew would never move. In those days, the sharp-money moves on the NBA totals were so strong that taking two points the worst of the opening number was nothing.

The adding machine—and I'm talking the very first ones made by Texas Instruments—was high science to Artichoke. When we won a bet with him, we often didn't cash for at least another week or so. When we picked up our money, he had each winning ticket filed away in an envelope containing the amount of the payout. It didn't matter if the ticket was worth $240 or $2.40. He had all the money accounted for this way, rather than pay out of a common till.

Back then, race books had the "house quinella." If you don't know, the quinella allows you to pick the first two horses to finish a race in either order. An "exacta" makes you pick the exact order of the first two finishers. An exacta is also figured directly from the pari-mutuel pool. The quinella, on the other hand, was a house bet where the price was determined by multiplying the win price (first place) times the place price (second place), then dividing by two. It was a tremendously popular bet. Of course, the wire service sent out the house quinella prices, but Artichoke never trusted them. He always wanted to check for himself.

That's why he used his "quinella machine" (an adding machine to sane people). He caught them rounding up a nickel instead of down on a couple quinellas a day. Yep. He must have saved a good two or three dollars in all the years he was in business by checking the actual price against what the wire service sent out.

When Artichoke Joe's finally closed its doors, he opened a card room in California. It seems that all the innovations in the sports world were just too much for him to keep up with.

✐ ✐ ✐

While I was running for Uncle Jack in 1979 and 1980, I got a list of games to bet. I had orders to bet them without checking with him, as long as the line was at the number or better. (Remember, this was long before cell phones.) If a game wasn't on the list, I got the line at each sports book I went to and we took it from there. The lines he gave me to bet right away were hard to find. I found some, but only once in a while.

Then one day … I went out with my marching orders, including the games to bet automatically. One of my first stops was Sam's Town. You remember that Sam's Town was taking bets from Uncle Jack and Lefty over the phone. This was a little before that time, so I still had to go in there on the square. But they were also about as sharp as you'd expect them to be.

The Raiders were playing the Chargers that day and Uncle Jack was looking to either lay 2½ on the Raiders or take the

Chargers +4. Sam's Town had the Raiders -2½. I made my bet and they took $5,000 to a side. Before I called Uncle Jack to report in, I waited to see if they were going to move the number.

They didn't.

"Yeah, Theo (Uncle in Greek), I'm at Sam's Town, you've got the Raiders minus two and a half for five dimes."

"Very good. Read me the rest of their line."

I read it, then told him they hadn't moved the Raiders number.

"Really? Well, bet 'em again."

I went to the same ticket writer, a guy who was a busted-out former bookmaker from Chicago. He knew about 10 times what the boss knew and I wanted to make sure he was aware I wasn't trying to pull anything by double-windowing the book. "I bet this before, but I'll take another five dimes on the Raiders minus two and a half."

Double-Windowing

An age-old battle between the bookmaker and the bettor is the attempted circumvention of betting limits. The books impose limits for risk management and protection against mistakes. On the other side, bettors who find a good situation want to bet as much as possible without moving the number.

One method of getting around the limit is known as "double-windowing." If the limit is $1,000, for example, a guy might bet $750 with one writer, then move to another window and bet it again. Or a team of two could hit two windows simultaneously. The advent of betting apps and kiosks introduced more ways to beat the limits, but the bookmakers countered with more stringent approval protocols. Requiring approval means that a big bet can be held up while someone surveys the situation before approving it.

"Yeah, he didn't move it," he told me, "so it's good."

He gave me the ticket and I waited another minute or two to see if the line moved. It didn't. I called Uncle Jack.

"Okay, you've got another five dimes on the Raiders minus two and a half."

"Great. Let me mark you down, Raiders minus two and a half for five more. That's a total of ten."

"Listen, Theo, I waited a couple minutes, but they still didn't move it."

"Yeah? Well, bet 'em again."

"Okay."

Same routine. I went to the same ticket writer, got to the front of the line, and told him, "I'll take the Raiders minus two and a half for another five dimes."

He shrugged. "I don't know what the hell he's doing back there, but he's had plenty of time to move it if he wanted to."

I made my bet and waited. Now I'd personally bet $15,000 on the Raiders -2½. They moved it and I called. "Okay, Theo, one more time, you've got the Raiders minus two and a half for another five dimes."

"Okay, let me mark you down. That's a total of fifteen thousand on the Raiders minus two and a half for Chris." He paused as he wrote. "So, did they move it?"

"Oh, yeah. They moved it."

He could hear the slight chuckle in my voice. "Don't tell me they moved it to three and a half?"

"Oh, no, they didn't move it to three and a half. They moved it to four."

"You're kidding me."

"No I'm not."

"Go bet 'em the Chargers plus four."

"I'll be right back."

I got in line, went to the same ticket writer, and before I

could even give him my bet, he looked at me and said, "I really don't know what the fuck he's thinking."

"Neither do I," I said, "but give me the Chargers plus four for five dimes."

I called Uncle Jack. "You've got the Chargers plus four for five dimes."

He started laughing. "What kind of idiots are running these joints?" It was a rhetorical question. This was a new brand of idiot. I'd like to say they're extinct, but they aren't. Some are still running Nevada sports books. In fact, one is the CEO of a multinational bookmaking concern. I'm not joking. Shows you how powerful 11/10 can be.

A few years later, one of Sam's Town's supervisors, Freddy White, came to work for me at the Cal Neva. He remembered the game and me betting it. He also remembered the guy who ran the joint bringing the supervisors around to show them that game on the computer screen.

Freddy told me, "He showed us and bragged, 'This is how you book a game.' It was way more action than we usually did on an NFL game.

"'Look at all this action. And we're booked perfectly. We can't lose.'

"I hated to tell him, but I did. 'No you're not. Do a what if, put in the Raiders winning by three, and see how perfectly you're booked.'

"Well, he did. He turned white. I thought he was going to vomit. He looked at us and said, 'Oh shit.' He never really knew what a middle was until that day."

By the way, do I even have to tell you? Final score: Raiders 24, Chargers 21.

✐ ✐ ✐

American journalist, satirist, critic, and skeptic H.L. Mencken said, "Nobody ever went broke underestimating the intelligence of the American people." I don't know if old H.L. was a book-maker, but he would have been a great one if he had been.

This particular story is about the all-time bad bet that I posted myself. The difference between this one and the rest of the tales in this chapter and the next is that I knew exactly what I was doing. I don't know if the devil made me do it or not, but let's just say that if he did, he only did it so he could make the players bet into it.

For years, I had customers ask me to book the Super Bowl coin flip. I could never understand it.

Why bet on a coin flip hundreds or thousands of miles away? I know it's the Super Bowl. So what? If you want to bet on a coin flip, pull a nickel out of your pocket and bet against one of these other guys who are dying to pick heads or tails. I'm sure not going to let you bet even money, so why would you lay juice on a bet that has absolutely no advantage on either side?

Year after year, I refused to put it up.

I booked Super Bowl-style props for every Monday Night Football game and did a lot of business on them every week and no one ever asked me to book the coin flip.

Somehow, now that the coin flip was associated with this particular game, everyone wanted to bet on it. It was completely idiotic.

Then one day … I finally relented.

I'd always prided myself on giving the bettors the best and fairest action they could find. I had the best odds on parlays, teasers, parlay cards, futures, and money lines. Whatever it was, I wanted the most action I could write and I would figure out a way to win a piece of it. But I felt this coin-flip bet was so stupid that I wanted to punish anyone dumb enough to want to bet on it. So I purposely put up the worst betting line of my life: heads -120/tails -120. That's right. If you were dumb enough to bet the coin flip, you were going to have to bet into a 40¢ line.

And what do you know? They bet the hell out of it. I did so much business on the thing I couldn't believe it. I had one guy even bet me $5,000. On a coin flip. With a 40¢ line. I'm thinking he had to have a trust fund. No one that dumb could have made enough money on his own to make change for a five-dollar bill.

I booked it every year after that and always did a ton of business. I did offer a better line after the first time, so I wasn't quite the prick I'd been. It's a mystery to me, but I had to keep my perspective and do what was best for my business.

And I always kept in mind the words of H.L Mencken. He was absolutely right.

Chapter 10

Adventures in Bad Bookmaking— Special Harrah's Edition

While making notes for my weekly podcast, I mentioned to Gill I wanted a Story Time with the theme, "Adventures in Bad Bookmaking."

Many stories came to mind, believe me; there's no shortage of terrible bookmakers. However, I noticed an inordinate amount came from one particular outfit: Harrah's. They were so bad, they deserved their own special segment on the podcast, and hence, their own chapter in this book.

I don't really know a proper metaphor. Let me just say that if a monument is ever built to bad bookmaking, it would have that Harrah's party script across the top. When it comes to bad bookmaking, Harrah's is Babe Ruth, Wayne Gretzky, Joe Montana, Secretariat, Vince Lombardi, John Wooden, Red Auerbach, and Michael Jordan all rolled into one. In other words, they're the greatest of all time.

Harrah's Reno is right across the street from Cal Neva. When I got there in 1981, our entire sports book consisted of two betting windows. We also had three windows in the race book and a cashier in the middle. The entire room housing all this couldn't have been more than 1,000 square feet.

Harrah's, on the other hand, was known throughout the country; their line was printed in a multitude of newspapers. The hotel had one of the first national, then international, reservations systems. Performers headlining the showroom were of the caliber of Bill Cosby, Bette Midler, Frank Sinatra, Joey Bishop, Sammy Davis, Jr., Red Skelton, Jay Leno, Don Rickles, and on and on. While I was at Cal Neva, B.B. King played *in the lounge!* They had a steakhouse that legitimately was one of the country's best restaurants, winning numerous awards over the years.

But if they ran their sports book with an ounce of common sense, Cal Neva would never have written a single bet. The sports book wouldn't even have existed.

A few days after I took over the sports book, Harrah's manager came by to introduce himself to me. He told me he wanted to be on friendly terms with the competition and that he and Scott Schettler, whom I replaced, were not. I told him, sure, that sounded good to me.

I'm a peacemaker at heart, though you might not believe it from reading this book. Especially this chapter. Nonetheless, I swear, I really am.

Scott isn't a peacemaker; he doesn't mind being confrontational. He can be a bit hotheaded at times, especially when he thinks he's in the right. I think he must have fired and rehired Roxy Roxborough about 100 times over the years. It took me a very short period of time to see why Scott didn't suffer the collection of fools at Harrah's sports book. In fact, my efforts toward a peaceful coexistence would soon vanish.

At that time, I had a pretty big personal betting bankroll, courtesy of Uncle Jack. Harrah's had two sports books, one in Reno, the other in Lake Tahoe, and each had its own separate line. There could be huge disparities in numbers due to a lack of communication and Tahoe was known to have some real doozies.

Then one day … I took a drive to the Lake on my day off to

see if I could find anything worth betting. This was a Tuesday, so the lines were mostly the openers at the three sports books there at the time. Even if I didn't find anything, it was early in the football season and I wanted to get the lay of the land. I was still a little tentative about the Reno people knowing too much about me, so I wanted to play at the Lake whenever possible just to stay a little secretive.

I went into Harrah's Tahoe and copied the line.

By the way, the other thing they did was put the plus sign next to the team on the board. If the Steelers were playing the Cowboys, instead of having the Steelers -3, they would list the Cowboys +3. It sounds simple enough, but it's confusing as hell when you're trying to write down the line as quickly as you can. The swing-shift casino manager at Cal Neva was an old Harrah's veteran. He tried to tell me everyone put up the pluses and I was the only one using the minus sign next to the team. Warren saw him questioning me and told him that I was running the sports book and he'd better keep to the rest of the casino. God bless Warren Nelson.

Uncle Jack always bet as much as the sports book would take. Thus, it was rare, almost unheard of, for me to bet less than the limit, whatever it might be. My standard procedure in a book, running bets for Uncle Jack, was to ask what the limits were. I was always polite (that's Chris the peacemaker); after all, I was looking to make a bet. I knew they set the rules. I just wanted to play as much as they'd let me.

So after copying the line, I asked the supervisor, "What do you take in football?"

He looked at me, gave me the once over, and replied, "Fifty thousand."

I shrugged and said, "Okay."

I went to the payphone, called Uncle Jack, and read him the line. "Okay," he said. "I don't see much, but Baylor looks playable at that number. Did you ask them what they take?"

"Yeah. The guy told me they take fifty thousand."

"Really?"

"That's what he told me."

"Well," Uncle Jack said, "I can't use fifty on that side, but I can use twenty. Bet them twenty thousand on Baylor."

"Okay."

This wasn't my first time betting or handling big money. I was young, but I was no rookie. Harrah's Lake Tahoe was a Four Diamond hotel, the only one in the country at that time, I believe. They catered to high rollers and put their line in every newspaper in the country as the "official" line. It wasn't true, but as far as I know, they might have believed their own bullshit.

I went into a stall in the bathroom and took money from the various places I had it hidden in my clothes. In those days when I carried large amounts of cash I wore a sport coat with lots of pockets, and a pair of shorts with lots of pockets under my outer pants. If I got robbed, I could empty one set of pockets and still have plenty left. I didn't want to lose it all to some creep with a gun. I counted out $22,000, put it in an easily retrievable pocket, and went to the window. That same supervisor was there and I gave the ticket writer my bet. "Twenty-two thousand to win twenty on number three-twenty-one Baylor."

"Whoa, whoa, whoa," the supervisor said. "What are you doing?"

I looked at the guy. I had no idea what he was talking about. "I'm making a bet," I said.

"You can't bet that much," he said.

"What do you mean, I can't bet that much?"

"We can't take a bet like that."

"What do you mean you can't take a bet like that? I just asked you what you take on the football and you told me fifty thousand. Now I'm betting you less than half that."

"You can have two thousand," he said.

"Two thousand? What the fuck?" Now I was getting pissed.

I'm getting pissed writing this, to tell you the truth. "Why did you tell me you took fifty thousand?"

Sports Speak

Like any other specialized activity, sports betting has phrases and language quirks that are all its own—unique even when compared to other forms of gambling.

For example, when talking about a specific sport, bettors and bookies like to insert "the" in front of it. So you'll hear, "Tommy comes in regularly to bet the hockey." To accept action is often expressed as "putting [someone] on," as in, "We put him on for the baseball." There's also the habit of speaking in the present tense, especially among bookmakers, from whom you might hear, "The Packers covered and we win ten grand." Or, "We lose five thousand on that play." Not "we won ten grand" or "we lost five thousand."

Another part of the lexicon is a special shorthand for money. Instead of betting $1,000, you bet a "dime," as in, "He bet two dimes on the Giants."

A bet of $500 is a "nickel." A bet of $100 is a "dollar." Of course, there are countless terms—e.g., "having gamble" (not afraid to take a shot), "stepping out" (making or taking a bet above your normal levels), "betting chalk" (wagering on the favorite), etc.—many of which are defined throughout this book. Probably the most common are the designations "sharp" and "square," the former referring to a skilled bettor and the latter to a casual bettor or the public. You'll hear "sharp/square money," "sharp/square play," "sharp/square lines," and on and on. Square sounds pejorative; I've always preferred using the term public rather than square.

"Well, I didn't think you wanted to bet that much."

"I came to you, asked you very politely, man to man, what you took on the football, and you treat me like some kind of asshole. What the fuck is wrong with you?"

"Look," he said, "you can have two thousand. Do you want it or not?"

"Yeah, I'll take it, but look what you did. You gave me a limit, I asked for forty percent of the limit, and you gave me ten percent of that. I had my money ready, twenty-two thousand pulled out in front of all these people. Now everyone in the joint knows how much money I have on me."

"Would you like an escort?"

"I don't need a fucking escort. What I need is for you to tell me what you take on a fucking bet and then take it. That's what I need."

"Well, next time I'll know."

"Why would you treat anyone like that? A person asks you a question, give him an answer. No need to be an asshole about it."

I made my bet and left. As far as I know, that guy is still there. Seriously, the last time I was there, he was still behind the counter. I'll say this, he found the perfect spot to make his career. I wish I could tell you that was a rare situation, but that's Harrah's standard operating procedure. Do you think it's easy blowing $28 billion? (That's what Caesars Entertainment, the renamed Harrah's corporation, was stuck before it emerged from bankruptcy, "only" $10 billion in the hole.) Oh, no. It takes work. It takes a team effort. Trust me, we're just getting started.

✎ ✎ ✎

In the days I was getting the line from Uncle Jack and Roxy, as a rule I used Uncle Jack's number for the game and Roxy's for the totals. I talked to both about any differences I saw, then we put our heads together and figured out the right number. I have to say, my numbers were about as good as any out there. After all, I was getting them from two of the best. I know people from all over the country were getting the line from the Cal Neva in those days. I don't blame them. It was about as good as it got.

As I mentioned, the media made it sound like the "official" football line came from Harrah's. It was complete and utter bullshit, but print and broadcast bought into it, proving once again they don't know a goddamned thing about our business. They didn't then and they don't now. I see the "experts" they quote and have on television and radio and most of us in the industry either laugh or cringe when these guys come on. They find an occasional good one, but mostly they haven't done a thing in the business except sell themselves well.

For an outfit that prided (read: sold) itself on being the opening line, the Harrah's managers unabashedly walked across the street, stood in front of my board, and copied my line every single day. That's not a joke or an exaggeration; they copied my line *every day*.

Then one day … in the early '80s, the Montreal Canadiens were the best team in the NHL. Back then, hockey games that were tied after regulation were just declared ties. There was no overtime period, no shootout if OT ended in a tie; the game simply ended and teams were each awarded a point in the standings. That was why plus or minus a half-goal was not only legitimate, but actually the most commonly used spread, because there wasn't necessarily a winner in every game like there is today. Of course, the money line was adjusted from there. If a game was essentially a pick 'em, we posted one team -½ and the other side minus the juice, like -150. If a team was -½ flat (when a number is quoted "flat," it means the lay price is the standard -110), usually the two teams were relatively even, but the home team was seen to have a half-goal home-ice advantage. If a team was -½ with juice on top of it, that was a superior team playing at home.

Well, this one day, the Canadiens were such big favorites, they were -1½ and -165. In a professional hockey game, it's almost unheard of for a team to be favored by two goals. We generally opened at about eight a.m. I remember it was the time of year where we had football, basketball, and hockey all going at once. I gave the line to the board man, then sat down at the computer to watch the action start coming in.

I looked up to see the guy from Harrah's copying the line as he did every day as the board man posted everything. I was monitoring the bets, making whatever moves I had to make, etc.—in other words, just a normal day at work.

At about nine o'clock, the action had slowed enough where I had a chance to check the board, running the line from my master sheet to check and see that all the line changes were made properly. Everything was done by hand in those days, so it was easy for a guy to miss something or make a mistake.

When I got to the hockey board, I noticed my guy had put up the Canadiens at -½ -165 instead of -1½ -165. Hockey betting was still essentially in its infancy, so no one had bet it and no one noticed, even though a one-goal difference in the line was monstrous. I told my guy to make the correction and he did. No big deal.

Usually, around 11 a.m., I had a little time to take a walk around town to stretch my legs and look in on the other sports books. Make no mistake, I was usually on the prowl for an off number that caught my eye, so I could make a personal bet. One never knew where any sports books might wind up after a morning of betting. This was long before the Internet, when bookmakers moved according to their business and not what they saw on a screen. Of course, they still had to know who was betting what to move numbers the way they were supposed to.

That, in the final analysis, was and is the art of bookmaking. That's the part the corporate guys with neckties and shiny shoes will never figure out.

Harrah's, of course, had no clue. After all, they were copying my line. What could they know? So, I usually stopped in there first.

As I walked in, the boss saw me, gave me the stink eye, went over to the board, and just erased the Canadiens' line. I never did see where he had it, but he'd opened it -½ -165, just like his guy had seen on my betting board. I probably would have bet if I'd seen it, but that wasn't my intention. I just started laughing, though he sure didn't think it was very funny. In fact, he was pissed at me like it was my fault, as if it was *my* responsibility for them to get the right number. I leaned over the counter and told him, "You know, you guys could get your own fucking line rather than just copying mine every day."

The Canadiens won that night, like they did almost every night. Good for them, and good for whoever bet them at Harrah's wrong line. I'm sure they lost a bundle on that game. Did they learn their lesson? Well, let's just say Harrah's had their guy in the Cal Neva the next day, copying the line like always.

🖋 🖋 🖋

One time Harrah's actually did open the line. No surprise: They fucked it up, just like you'd expect them to. Of all the Harrah's stories, this is the most unbelievable, but I swear every word of it is true.

In 1987, the NFL owners locked out their players. The owners took an exceptionally hard stand. It wasn't enough that their franchises' values were growing exponentially, while they bilked the public out of money for building stadiums, or that the players' careers end in their early 30s and they get their brains scrambled or their joints ruined, so they wanted as much money as they could get their hands on while they were still healthy enough to make it. No, that wasn't enough. The owners wanted more, which meant paying the players less.

I don't cry for players in any of the major sports leagues—except for football. Those guys put their bodies on the line to play this game for our enjoyment and they have the worst situation of all the athletes from the major sports. Their contracts aren't guaranteed, but what is guaranteed is their bodies will be in ruins if they have any kind of a lengthy career.

The owners knew they were going to lock out the players and formed replacement teams. If you're too young to remember this, it sounds like fiction. In fact, a movie was made about it, but it's all true. For the most part, these were guys who couldn't play a lick; for example, they were cut out of training camp and, under normal circumstances, had no shot of ever playing in the league. And don't forget, to play in one of these replacement games meant you had to cross a picket line. Most true borderline guys didn't want to cross. Many didn't, but some did. Mostly those were ex-football players who were doing something else. I remember one guy was a rodeo cowboy who had played for Wyoming or Montana years before; now he was a starting linebacker in the NFL. A couple of star football players, Joe Montana and Danny White most notably, did cross the picket lines.

Some teams were tremendously prepared, while others did almost nothing before kickoff time in the first replacement games and had to scramble for players up to the last minute. These games all counted in the standings, (which I'll talk about more in the "Mental Cruelty" chapter).

Rosters were almost impossible to come by. The actual NFL players who did cross the picket lines weren't announced until just before the games. They were being pressured to stay in line with the union. Many made last-minute decisions one way or the other.

With just a few days before the games, no one, and I mean *no one*, had a line on any of them. But guess who decided to open the very first lines. You're probably way ahead of me. Of course, you've got it by now. Harrah's.

I was in the sports book on Tuesday morning when Jimmy Chang, one of my customers, walked in. At this point, he was in Reno, just starting to become successful. In a few years, the whole betting world would know how sharp he was, but for the time being, it was just us Reno bookmakers who were getting killed by Jimmy.

As I've said, I never chased wiseguys or their action. I kept them to their limits and tried to manipulate the line to go in with their sides whenever possible. Of course, I couldn't do that all the time, but I could do it often enough where it was worth it to me to keep a good relationship with them. So Jimmy and I became good friends, even going to dinner together on occasion.

He came up to the counter and called me over. "Chris, look at these," he said while showing me a handful of betting slips from Harrah's. They were the NFL replacement games. He'd bet practically every underdog on the board for a dime a piece.

"What the hell?" I shook my head. "They can't possibly be booking these."

"Yes! They're on the board right now!"

I looked at his tickets. There was absolutely no rhyme or reason to any number. The only possible explanation was that they pulled the numbers right out of their ass. More charitably, if that's possible, in their arrogance, they believed that by putting up a number, the public would just feel they knew something no one else did.

They actually thought they could pull something like this off. Dumb and arrogant is a dangerous combination. One team was a 7-point road favorite, some games were pick 'em, others had the home teams as double-digit chalk (chalk means the favorite;

double-digit chalk means a big favorite), and so on. Jimmy told me they moved all the numbers after he bet, but they were still well worth playing. I sent someone over and pretty much bet the whole board, usually taking about a point worse than Jimmy had gotten, but it was still highway robbery.

Chalk

The term "chalk" is believed to have originated from the days when sports books posted lines on chalkboards and wrote the spreads next to the favorites. So rather than write something like Packers -3 and Bears +3, they put a -3 next to the Packers or simply "Packers 3." Due to this convention, the favorite was indicated by the (extra) chalk. Even though today's boards are electronic, the old-time procedure still prevails and provides a trick for reading lines: You can easily determine the favorite in a game by glancing at the board and noting next to which team the pointspread number is positioned.

After I got all the plays down, I called John Falenski, who was working for me at the time. John is out of the business right now, which is too bad. In all my years as a bookmaker, I've never met a better judge of football talent. No one ever came close. And he wasn't only a whiz with talent, he could translate that into creating a value to place on a player or a roster of players.

Now remember, no one knew a damn thing at this point about who was even playing for and against whom. The rosters were just barely starting to emerge and for some unknown reason, Harrah's was the only line in the entire world.

"John, if you had to make a number on these replacement games, what would you make them?" I put the question to him over the phone.

"Impossible. You can't make a number. No one knows who's playing."

"John, if someone had a gun to your head and said you had to make a number, what would you make them?"

By now he was getting aggravated. The whole thing was stupid. That was my point. "Get the fuck out of here. It's just ridiculous."

"John. Gun to your head. What do you make them?"

Really exasperated, he shut me down with, "Home teams minus two."

"Exactly!"

At that point, there really wasn't any other number you could make. Home teams -2 was probably the closest you could come to anything reasonable.

"Listen to these plays I got from Harrah's," I said and started listing the plays.

"You've got to be kidding me."

"No. And not only that, I missed the good numbers. Jimmy Chang beat me in and got better numbers than I got."

"Holy shit!"

"Find rosters and come up with numbers for each of these games. I'll give you a piece of anything I get."

"You got it. It might take me a couple days, but I'll see what I can find."

John did his homework. We didn't lose a bet that week. I bet them all straight and gave John a piece of everything I collected. He was so right on with everything, it was a joke. Even the one or two games Harrah's stumbled in on the right side got moved enough where we had middles going for us. John wound up parlaying all our plays where the numbers were still playable and hit a 9-teamer. It was a thing of beauty.

One more little side note of Harrah's being Harrah's. By the third week, the numbers had kind of settled in, with some uniformity around the betting world. I was walking through

Harrah's and they had a number I liked. It wasn't outrageous, just a half-point better than anywhere else. I approached the counter and working there was this one girl who really hated me. I mean, she just despised me. Nonetheless, she was the only one working. I tried to be nice.

Honest I did.

"What are you taking on the NFL games?"

"A dime," she said.

"Perfect. I just want a nickel on the Saints plus three and a half."

"You can have three dollars," she said.

"What the fuck? I asked you what the limit is, you tell me, I only want to bet half that, and you cut me to three dollars. Why do you do that?"

"Do you want the three dollars or don't you?"

Honest to God, I don't know how they train these people to be such total assholes, but it sure as hell works.

🖋 🖋 🖋

In the late '80s, Harrah's started a promotion with its new slogan: "The Better People Place."

Stop and think. How arrogant is that? *The Better People Place?* Are you kidding? They're saying the people everywhere else are some sort of lesser human than the people at their glorious casinos.

It took them awhile, but they finally figured out how condescending that was. My goodness, how can they be so clueless? Like I've been saying, do you think it's easy to blow $28 billion? It isn't. It takes one hell of an effort. But this outfit was up to the task.

🖋 🖋 🖋

From the early '80s to the early '90s, Joe Montana and the San Francisco 49ers tortured bookmakers everywhere. With San Francisco just over the hill, no one bore the brunt of this more than the Reno sports books. The 49ers won four Super Bowls during that stretch, which was bad enough, but they were also winning and covering almost every week. Most of those games went over the total, too. The rule of thumb is that the public loves to bet on the favorite and the over, so square bettors were having a picnic. It was a broken record: "I'll bet the Niners for a nickel to pay for my trip. I'll parlay them to the over to make a little extra." Most of the time, Bay Area sports bettors were getting everything, essentially, for free. Meanwhile, I was the biggest bookmaker in Reno at the time, so guess who was taking the brunt of the brunt? You got it.

Still, I wasn't complaining. In the first place, how many do you think went home with money in their pockets? Not many. The public always figures out a way to blow their money. Secondly, as you know by now, I was Chris "Bring on the Action" Andrews. If the numbers are right, I'll figure out how to make it work. And thirdly, when the newspapers asked me about it once, my answer was, "These people come to our town, put money in our slot machines, play our table games, and eat in our restaurants. If they get a winner on the Forty-Niners, good for them. I hope they come back next week."

When Leon Nightingale, who was chairman of the board at Cal Neva, read it, he singled me out in a management meeting and told the whole company that this was the attitude we wanted to display at Cal Neva. Mr. Nightingale became one of my biggest fans. And I became one of his. As I've mentioned several times, there was often a lot of drama among the partners at Cal Neva, with Warren Nelson and Leon on opposite sides, but they were both awfully good to me.

In the same newspaper article, Harrah's came off pissing and moaning about how the 49er bettors were kicking their ass every week. I remember wondering at the time if that was also part of Harrah's training. But while Harrah's was chasing out the winners, we were inviting them in. My business was growing exponentially and theirs, well, they weren't stuck $28 billion for the hell of it.

One of the all-time chicken-shit things Harrah's did was on their futures book. They not only had the lowest price in town on the 49ers to win the Super Bowl, they also had them -4½ *in the Super Bowl!* That's right. Not only did your futures bet need them to win the Super Bowl, they had to cover 4½ in the Big Game. Why didn't they just put up a sign telling guys who wanted to bet on their local team to stick it up their ass?

Oh wait, that's right, they did have a sign! I'll get to that shortly.

✏ ✏ ✏

If Nevada sports books ever want to take back their place in the upper echelon of sports betting from the offshore books, one place they can start is by offering better futures odds. Futures odds are the odds of winning an event in the future. It could be a long way off, like betting on the winner of the Super Bowl before the teams even go to summer training camp. Futures can also be betting on the auto race or golf tournament for the coming weekend. There are one or two places in the entire state that give you a fair bet on futures. I've always loved booking futures, but most of these guys are scared to death. With the bar set so low, Harrah's can still crawl under it like a limbo champion. No bar can be set low enough for the Better People Place.

Prior to the 2001 baseball season, Alex Rodriguez left the Seattle Mariners as a free agent to sign with the Texas Rangers. A-Rod was considered the best player in baseball and when he signed the richest contract in sports history, the futures money poured in on the Rangers to win the World Series. Of course, the

Rangers still had absolutely no pitching and certainly couldn't afford to acquire any now that A-Rod was taking such a big chunk of their payroll.

Like any intelligent bookmaker, we took money on the Rangers and moved the line accordingly.

One lesson lost on many bookmakers is that when you lower one team's odds, you should raise another's. Whatever the futures prop is, one team will win and all the rest will lose. You want to make enough off the losers to pay off the winner.

Sounds simple and it is. Still, most corporate bookmakers in Nevada don't get it.

A-Rod didn't make much of a difference for the Rangers. They won 71 games in 2000 and 73 games in 2001, a gain of two games. Pretty poor return for $25 million a year. Meanwhile, the Mariners went from 91 wins in 2000 to 116 wins in 2001, a gain of 25 games by *losing* A-Rod.

Before the season started, the Rangers were bet down at Harrah's to 3-1 to win the World Series. Most sports books, even though they faded the same flood of money, had the bet at about 5-1, but offering a worse price than anyone else's is one more thing Harrah's is famous for.

The Rangers and Mariners were in the same division and vying for the same playoff spot. At one point in the season, the Rangers were 50 games behind the Mariners. *Fifty games!* Yet Harrah's never changed the odds on the Rangers. I usually kept my mouth shut when they did ridiculous things, but this time I just couldn't hold back.

"You should be ashamed of yourselves," I said while all three guys who ran the book were standing there. "The Rangers are fifty games out and you have them three-to-one to win the World Series. Not play five-hundred ball, not sneak into the playoffs somehow—no, three-to-one to win the World Series."

"Well, we have a lot of money on them," one of those geniuses replied.

"No shit. Everyone does. I don't care how much you have on them. They're almost mathematically eliminated. That's an absolutely ridiculous price."

Sure, there was the wild card playoff spot. It's true that they could have gotten into the post-season without overtaking the Mariners. However, in case you're interested, the Rangers finished 27 games out of the wild-card spot, too.

🖋 🖋 🖋

In the late '90s, Harrah's moved its sports book into the old bingo parlor, a huge room downstairs. Word leaked out about how well the remodel was going, especially the sandwich counter and a bar with a terrific selection of draft beers, which is tremendously appealing to sports bettors. They had televisions everywhere for both the sports and the race books. Some of the construction workers were coming over to the Cal Neva after their shift and filling us in on the progress. It promised to be the nicest sports book in Reno, if not the entire state.

On the day of the opening, I went in to take a look, just like every other sports bettor in town. Descending the escalators to the new book, I could hear the festivities. I saw champagne and hors d'oeuvres that were free to the public with some pretty sharp-looking cocktail waitresses to serve them. It was a party atmosphere all the way around.

Then I saw the 15-foot-long banner that met everyone at the bottom of the escalator. It hung from the ceiling and was strung across the length of the sports book counter. It read, "We Reserve The Right To Refuse Any Wager." This was their greeting. This was the message they wanted to send as your first impression as you entered this multimillion-dollar renovation.

Honest to god, you can't make this shit up. The first thing they wanted everyone to know was that no matter what, they were still going to run out any customer who had a clue about how to do anything but donate their money to Harrah's.

It took a few days, but someone had them take the banner down. I guess whoever that was gets some kind of kudos. But really, how could they be so clueless in the first place?

🖋 🖋 🖋

By now you get the picture, though I could write an entire book about Harrah's by itself. Still, one more story has to be told. No Harrah's history could be complete without it.

In the Chicago Bears' Super Bowl season of 1985, my cousin Archie was working at Caesars Palace. He put up the very first Super Bowl prop: "Will William 'The Refrigerator' Perry score a touchdown?"

Perry was the heaviest player in the league at the time and the Bears used him occasionally in goal-line situations. It seemed like a gimmick. If the Bears were in a tight game, they almost surely wouldn't put in the Fridge to score a vital touchdown. You could bet only that he would score; there was no way to bet that he wouldn't.

The bets poured in on the Fridge to score. The Bears blew out the Patriots that day. Bears' Coach Mike Ditka called for Perry to get the ball at the goal line and he scored. To this day, I think Ditka did it just to screw Vegas—in this case "Vegas" was my cousin Archie.

Don't shed too many tears for Archie; he's doing fine. Caesars overcame their losses, too. I'd say they were doing fine too and they were—until Harrah's bought them years later. Now they're part of the multi-billion dollar losses. Archie and Caesars took a bath on that particular wager, but a whole new market opened up from it: proposition wagering. I wrote how I've invented a few wagering options and I'm very proud of that. But it should be noted my cousin came up with this one and it's grown to be a monster. This past Super Bowl, the props took in more money than the game itself. Good on ya, Archie.

So proposition (prop) betting took off. It started with the basics, such as bets on the individual quarters and halves, field goals, and interceptions. It eventually grew to all sorts of things, like incorporating other sports (would Michael Jordan score more points in his game than one of the teams in the Super Bowl), the announcers saying certain catchphrases, or the length of the national anthem.

When new options are available for betting, inevitably some mistakes are made. God knows, I made a few in my day. But a certain sports book made a mistake that topped them all. Guess which.

I wish I could remember the exact details, but I'm fairly certain this was in the AFC and NFC championships, which decided the Super Bowl teams. Harrah's put out a parlay card on the games with the pointspread and the total, the first and second halves with the pointspread and total, and each individual quarter with the pointspread and total.

All these props were being booked as straight betting options, so the numbers were all right in line. That wasn't the problem. Unless you're a veteran gambler, you might not see what's wrong. Don't feel bad. The guy who ran the sports book at the Better People Place didn't see what was wrong either.

Let me explain. I'll keep the examples very simple and stick to the game total, because that's where all the trouble was.

If the total for the game is 48, then the first-half total would be 24 and the second half total would be 24. The first quarter would be a total of 10, the second quarter would be 14. The third quarter would be 10 and the fourth quarter 14. Those are very rough numbers, so if you have complaints about their accuracy, I really don't care. I'm trying to keep this simple.

These numbers were all available to bet straight as well. There was no steam from the wiseguys making straight bets, so everything seemed fine. However, these were on a parlay card, so not only *could* you parlay them, you *had to* parlay them on this particular card. The card went out and they thought since all the numbers looked solid, there would be no problem taking all the action people wanted.

Steam

The term "steam"—used in the context of a "steam play" or a "steam move"—describes a game where the line is moving as a result of the wiseguys coming in heavily on one side. Word may have gotten out that someone has inside information or that a prominent player has bet a game. The line moves on that steam and others begin jumping on the moving train. Over the years, the infamous sports bettor Billy Walters has been the main source of steam plays in Nevada. However, today, others in the market are well-respected for their betting prowess and can create steam.

As a bookmaker, I give plays from a respected player a solid move. I'll move a football game off a key number (3 or 7) or move it a whole point, which I would never do based on a big bet from an unknown player. The public loves to bet steam, but what they don't understand is that if a wiseguy lays 6 on a game and now they're jumping in at -7, it's not nearly the same thing as what the wiseguy bet.

The action started coming in. It was normal at first, and then it started picking up. Then it *really* picked up.

Here was the problem. If the first quarter went over 10 and the second quarter went over 14, the first half would go over 24. If the first quarter went under 10 and the second quarter went under 14, the first half would go under 24. If the first half went over 24 and the second half went over 24, then the game would go over 48. If the first half went under 24 and the second half went under 24, then the game would go under 48. In its simplest form, by betting the first half over 24 to the second half over 24, then parlaying that to the game over 48, you were betting a 2-team parlay and getting paid for a 3-team parlay. Or you could bet the first half under 24 to the second half under 24 and parlay that to the game under 48. Same difference: If you hit the first two, you got paid for a 3-teamer.

Instead of getting paid for a parlay that figured 13/5 or +260, you earned 5/1 or +500. Carry it out further and the odds are even greater in the bettor's favor. You could put together 4-team parlays that would pay out like a 6-teamer, so you'd get 40-1 instead of 20-1. Six-teamers would be paid like 9-teamers, 250-1 instead of 40-1. If all four quarters went the same way, you could win and get paid for a 9-team parlay by parlaying all the quarters to the two halves and the game. Those are odds of 10-1 that are getting paid 250-1!

There were two games with those types of props. We wheeled everything that was correlated within a game and had dozens of parlays ranging all the way up to 9-teamers. The wiseguys figured it out and were betting all the possibilities as quickly as they could fill out the cards.

Now, here's the thing. You didn't have to win. The outcomes could and did split out often. In other words, the first half score could go over 24 and the second half under 24, but at that point, it didn't matter if you bet over or under for the game, because the correlation was broken. Even though you could lose, if you bet those correlations often enough, you'd eventually break the casino. The math holds up. You could and would lose and lose fairly often. However, over the long run, the odds were *drastically* in favor of the player.

Well, after getting flooded with action, Harrah's managers realized something was wrong. Finally, someone put two and two together and figured out the problem. They halted all the action and wanted everyone to turn their cards back in for a refund. Yeah. Like that would happen. It sounds like the guys who came up with Mitt Romney's idea of self-deportation.

Then Harrah's put out the word that whoever didn't turn in their cards would be banned for life from betting. Employees who didn't turn them in would be summarily fired. Of course, if anyone hit a card, how hard would it be to get someone to cash it for you? Lots of people bet, but a lot of people don't. Finding a beard would not be a problem.

Wouldn't you know it? The games split out. They definitely got lucky and either didn't lose or actually made a little bit of money. Otto Bismarck said, "God looks out for drunks and fools." Well, just let me say I would never accuse the bookmakers at Harrah's of being drunks.

✐ ✐ ✐

Later in my career, after the Cal Neva, when I was informed that I was no longer employed by the Golden Nugget, I was contacted by someone at Harrah's to possibly be part of its sports book management team. I said I'd would think about it. I went home and told my wife Pam, who knew all about Harrah's foibles and how I felt about their operation.

"You won't last fifteen minutes," she said. "You won't get through the first five minutes of the interview before you snap. Are you crazy? You can't do that."

Of course, she was right. They were too far gone for me to pull them out of it. The only chance they would have is to allow a third party to come in and run their sports books. Now, if some folks put together a group to manage them as a satellite operation, that's something I could be interested in. Harrah's, the ball is in your court.

Chapter 11

"The Last Thing We Gotta Worry About Is Running Out of Money"

I saw innumerable systems bettors at the Cal Neva, but one pair of fairly young gamblers showed up during the 1982 baseball season.

The Minnesota Twins were coming off a dismal season, going 41-68 (.376) in the strike-shortened 1981 campaign. They'd also been last in the American League in attendance and their television revenues were minimal. The projections of the Twins being the worst team in baseball were coming true, with only mild competition from other quarters.

On May 5, 1982, the Twins were treading water at 10-17. It was pretty clear things would soon get worse. Roxy Roxborough and I discussed how we weren't posting the Twins as big enough underdogs every day. When they were on the road, they ordinarily got +190 or +200. Roxy felt they should be +280 or even more. Even at home, the Twins were the underdogs, usually coming in around +130. Roxy felt they should be much higher, like +180 or +190. According to the market, however, the prices were usually settling in where Roxy thought they were wrong. He convinced me that he was right and I started opening the Twins with bargain prices that enticed the wiseguys.

I can't swear to the exact date, but in late May, two guys came to the Cal Neva, one in his early 30s, the other in his late 20s. They were interested only on betting one team, the Twins.

They put up the limit of $2,000 on their first bet and when I moved the number, they asked if they could get $3,000. No problem. I moved it again and they bet another $2,000. They never looked at any other games. They were polite and cheery, got done with their business, and were on their way.

The Twins lost that night, of course, but the next day, these two bettors came in with the exact same m.o. Only this time, they bet $4,000 at the third number (I learned well from my days at the Barbary Coast).

The Twins lost again, yet there they were again the next day. They weren't interested in any other game, they just started betting the Twins. I told them once I got to the third number, they could bet whatever they wanted. We had a good group of wiseguys hanging around the Cal Neva at that time and I could move as much as I wanted the other way, so putting them on was no problem. This time they bet $6,000 on the last number.

This was three days in a row and, needless to say, this wasn't what ordinary customers were looking for. I had to probe a little. "Do you guys mind if I ask you what you're doing?"

The older one answered. "We'll tell you as long as you promise not to screw around with the lines."

"That's an easy one," I said. "I have no trouble getting as much action as I want back on the other side."

"Well," the older one again did the talking. "We're going to keep betting the Twins every day. We know they have to win sooner or later and they're big dogs every day. We keep pressing our bets, so when they do win, we'll get all our money back and then some."

The two had big smiles on their faces like they just figured out how to print money legally.

"That makes a lot of sense," I said. "The only problem is

you might run out of money before they actually win a game."

The guy looked me right in the eye (honest to God, I'll never forget this if I live to be 1,000 years old) and said, "The last thing we gotta worry about is running out of money."

I just shrugged my shoulders and said, "Okay."

The Twins lost again. And again. And again.

True to their word, the two guys were in every day and pressing. Some of my customers told me they were brothers from an oil family in Texas. They figured the two somehow got into Daddy's money and figured out a "can't-lose" scheme that would make a bit of dough for themselves and put the money back as soon as they made their profit.

Meanwhile, the Twins' losing streak hit 17 games. The brothers were there for at least 14 of the losses. On June 4, the Twins finally won, but the brothers weren't around.

The next day, there they were again. "Can you believe it?" They were incredulous. "The one day we couldn't make it, the Twins finally win?"

It really *was* unbelievable.

This is 100% true. I couldn't make this up. It was like a scene from a bad movie. Their clothes were disheveled and their hair was greasy and messed up like they were coming off a night of some serious drinking. The word I got was they had to go back to Texas to pick up more money. I never found out if they fessed up to Daddy at that point or not.

The Twins then lost another five straight and the brothers were there for every one of them. When the Twins won again, they were gone. This time for good. They disappeared, never to be seen by me (at least in person) again.

We didn't have all of today's cash-transaction reporting back then, so I'm not exactly sure how much they blew, but it had to be well over $300,000 and probably closer to $500,000. And that was just at the Cal Neva, by the way. But in the end, I was booking all their action. The other guys in town were scared off by then. (I told you I learned well at the Barbary Coast.) I booked it the way I was taught and kept a couple positions for myself every night. We probably made more than $150,000 off their system, but by creating that kind of action, it was one more step in building our business.

I learned early on if you're a drug addict or an alcoholic, you can only abuse yourself so much before you wind up dead. If you're going through money, though, and have the access, you can blow as much as they print. I also learned that when you're playing a system, be prepared for the craziest things in the world to happen. I don't know of any "can't-lose" system. None. Zero. The only real can't-lose systems will put you in jail. I call jail a loser, but that's just me.

Finally, I learned don't ever, *ever*, EVER tempt the gambling gods. I already knew it, but this little escapade confirmed it. Not only do those gods get pissed off real easy, but they don't like it when you make fun of them. So they'll make you pay. You will definitely pay.

The two brothers are probably back in the family's good graces by now. I'm sure they have a laugh at their folly in an earlier life, thinking how they had a scheme that couldn't possibly backfire, but of course it did. They're probably on a yacht or in a mansion, sipping Dom Perignon, and wondering whether to have the crab, the lobster, or both for dinner.

Heck, the older one might even be thinking about the eight years he spent in the White House.

Chapter 12

Mental Cruelty

It didn't take long for the Cal Neva to start getting a reputation as a sports book that was willing to take a bet. The casino had already established itself as a place for real gamblers, the kind you don't see that often anymore. The casino landed the sports book our first whale.

He was a successful businessman and a minor celebrity in the region of the country where he lived. I wish I could tell you more, because it would really add to the story, but I can't. I can tell you that he was a degenerate gambler. Man, was he a degenerate gambler.

"Ben" started playing with us by betting football. He always bet the limit, then parlays with his sides, coming back after we moved the number for more action and pressing his bets at the half, never hedging back a penny. Ben also fired away in the pit. He loved blackjack and the Cal Neva had the most liberal rules in Nevada. He took a whole table, playing the limit on up to seven hands at a time. It didn't take long to see he was no wiseguy.

Bill McHugh was the casino manager at the time. He eventually became general manager, president, and CEO. Bill loved this guy's action. Usually, guys like Ben were good at sports and blew it in the pit. Ben was the opposite. He was a pretty good blackjack player and we usually nailed him in the sports book.

Once, Ben was late with his flight connections getting to town, but wanted to bet a college basketball game. It was an early-season game between BYU and UCLA, a pretty big match-up that was on national television. It was coming up to halftime and I don't think Ben had even checked into his room yet. This was the mid-'80s, there was no Internet, and no one was booking halftimes in college basketball. Nonetheless, Ben told me that if I made him a halftime line, he'd guarantee me a $30,000 bet. That's the kind of player he was. You might think he really was watching the game and saw an injury or something, but that wasn't his m.o. God knows he pulled plenty of other shit, but that wasn't the way he tried to scam.

Ben's usual bets were anywhere from $20,000 to $50,000. Every once in a while, he bet $100,000. He was obviously a sharp businessman, but he wasn't much on money management in the sports book. He was always pressing his bets late in the week before heading home, win or lose. Of course, he bested us at times, but that's not a solid strategy for winning money long term.

We had Ben as a customer for a couple years.

Then one day … in the 1987 football season, there was a Sunday night game between the Chicago Bears and the Minnesota Vikings.

The Bears had won the Super Bowl after the 1985 season with one of the best teams in NFL history. They were now two years removed from that win. Though the Bears were still good enough to win their division, they were in decline from the great '85 team. However, in the eyes of the betting public, they still garnered much respect, mostly from what that championship team had accomplished.

The 1987 season was a strike year. As I wrote in Chapter 9, when the players went out on strike, the NFL owners put together replacement teams. Some teams did a good job at it and some didn't. The Vikings were one of the teams that didn't.

Once the strike was settled, the NFL wiped the statistical records of any players who participated in those travesties, but the three games played during the strike counted in the standings. The Vikings were one of the NFL's best teams, but found themselves in desperate straits because they had lost all three replacement games.

This Sunday-night game between two teams from the same division fighting for playoff positions was a big one for both sides. The game was a pick, with pretty even money on both sides.

Ben had come up for the weekend with a cashier's check for $275,000. After breaking dead-even for the weekend, he put $220,000 to win $200,000 on the Vikings.

At this point, we decided not to book his action in the traditional way, by moving the number and trying to arbitrage it with the rest of the betting public. Instead, we just booked it all ourselves, win or lose. But I never told him that. When Ben came in to make his bet, the game was pick 'em. It was shortly before kickoff and there was no way to offset his bet with other action, even if I wanted to, which I didn't. Like I said, I didn't want to let him know any of that.

Negotiating with Ben often meant walking a fine line. We wanted all of his action, but of course we wanted to book it in a way that was most advantageous to us. While there was no real competition for his business in Reno, he could easily go to Vegas. He wouldn't be quite the whale he was in Reno, but this guy was a big fish no matter where he went. Cal Neva didn't have fancy restaurants or rooms of any kind, so all we really had were the willingness and ability to take his action. Had Ben ever gone to see Jimmy Vaccaro at the Mirage, Jimmy would have fixed him up with a suite, comps at the finest restaurants, etc. But he would have been just one more big player to Jimmy. To us, he was a monster. And I think he liked that.

I got Ben to lay pick 'em for half his bet and -1 for the other half. I told him I had to have something to show Bill McHugh that I didn't just get trampled by him, and since it was so close to game time, he left me little choice but to demand that split line. In all honesty, at that point I don't really think Bill cared about moving the number on him. I just wanted to put us in a better position for the action.

At halftime, the Bears had a 13-7 lead. Ben came back and put the other $55,000 to win $50,000 on the Vikings. It was one of those things where I knew he was going to bet it. There was no way he was going to head home without putting every penny of that cashier's check into action.

Both starting quarterbacks got hurt during the game. The Viking starter, Tommy Kramer, had been in and out of the lineup with injuries all season. His backup was the more-than-capable veteran Wade Wilson.

The Bears weren't in that good of a position. Jim McMahon was Chicago's flamboyant quarterback. No one was neutral on their opinions of McMahon. Some saw him as a nut, a cad, a mercurial leader, a moron, a swashbuckler, a guy you'd go to war with or a guy you couldn't stand to be around. No one could deny his style fit the Bears perfectly and they wouldn't be the same team without him.

McMahon's backup was undrafted third-year man Mike Tomczak. Tomczak had a good, but not great, career at Ohio State. Nonetheless, no team thought he was worth a draft choice. While McMahon was the Bears starter, he had suffered occasional injuries. The Bears had gone through high-profile backups who never seemed to quite fit the bill. They tried former first-round draft choice Steve Fuller, Heisman Trophy winner Doug Flutie, future Super Bowl winning coach Sean Payton, first-round draft choice (and another future successful coach) Jim Harbaugh. The unheralded Tomczak beat them all out.

Tomczak spent a few years with the Bears, then went on to the Packers and Browns. He finished his career with seven years as a Steeler, where he also had some success. He was never anything but a competent quarterback, but if you watch enough NFL football, that's not always the easiest thing in the world to find. Tomczak stuck around the NFL for 15 seasons. In 1996, he was the unquestioned starter for a 10-6 Steeler team that went to the playoffs. As a starter, his teams were 42-31. The guy wasn't bad.

I sure as hell didn't know all that when he took McMahon's place in a game I needed for more than a quarter of a million dollars.

McMahon led the Bears to an early third-quarter touchdown, making it 20-7 Bears. I didn't think we were home free, but I was feeling pretty good. Bill and I were watching the game together in his office. We'd sectioned off a separate area of the sports book so Ben could watch it by himself. We also had a camera on him, though I'm not sure he knew about it.

Ben wasn't exactly the coolest calmest guy when he was losing. When the Bears went up 20-7, he was throwing a fit, along with newspapers and even ashtrays. He was smoking cigarettes like he was about to face the firing squad.

Our hopes for an easy win quickly went down the drain. Wade Wilson hit Vikings star receiver Anthony Carter for a 60-yard touchdown pass and on the next possession, he connected with Carter again, this time for a 35-yard touchdown. By the end of the third quarter, the Vikings had gone ahead 21-20. Then they kicked a field goal to extend their lead to 24-20. The Bears also kicked a field goal to cut it to 24-23. McMahon sustained an ankle injury and was now watching from the sideline.

The Bears got the ball back with less than two minutes to play, down by one, with Mike Tomczak at the helm instead of Jim McMahon. The season before, Tomczak had thrown for two touchdowns and 10 interceptions while playing for the injured McMahon. I was less than confident.

Forcing Ben to lay -1 for half his original bet made me look like a sharp bookmaker, but that wasn't what I wanted right then. Even though it looked like he was going to win the first $100,000 bet and another $50,000 on the halftime, Ben would be pissed that the -1 portion of the split wager would result in a tie. He was the kind of guy who could see a gray cloud in any silver lining. I didn't want to lose him as a customer, so this was now the worst of both worlds—I was going to blow $150,000 and have a pissed-off customer on my hands. On the other hand, ideally, we would win the bet and not have to worry about any of that shit.

Meanwhile, Tomczak had the Bears on the move. It was fourth down and the Bears had the ball at the Vikings' 38-yard line. It would have been a 55-yard field-goal attempt from there, but Bears' coach Mike Ditka left the offense on the field.

Tomczak went back to pass; the flow of the play was all to the right. As everyone was going right, Dennis Gentry lined up in the right slot and ran a short pattern to the left. Tomczak hit Gentry with the pass, hoping to get the first down and put the Bears in a position to kick a field goal. Vikings linebacker Ashley Ambrose was trailing Gentry on the play. He dove at his ankles to make the tackle and missed. I remember there being a weird angle from the television camera, but you could see it right away. Gentry was gone. He strolled into the end zone and gave the Bears a 30-24 win.

Bill and I were in the office going nuts.

Ben was in the sports book going nuts.

Our nuts were a lot better than his. He tore the joint up, tossing papers, ashtrays, chairs, anything he could get his hands on. We watched him go to the house phone. He called the operator and demanded to speak to Bill. Bill made him sweat a little (that was kind of fun to watch), then finally answered. He wanted to cash a check for $20,000 and go play blackjack.

Bill went to meet him in the pit and I went to the sports book. I had to check the figures. We were still growing our business and this was the biggest day we'd ever had. I snuck back down to the pit area, but stood off to the side. I knew he was furious at everyone, especially Bill and me, so I stayed out of sight. I wanted to watch his blackjack action, though. He was the kind of guy who had a chance to get it all back and I didn't want that. Bill sectioned off an area of the pit especially for Ben and brought in a dealer I knew. He was the calmest dealer you ever met, a real quiet cerebral type. What he was doing dealing, I'll never know. The game began. If the dealer had a face card showing and Ben got dealt anything like a 12 or 14, Ben took his cards, ripped them up, and threw them at the dealer.

My dealer buddy never flinched. He just looked over to the pit boss and said, "New deck." I was watching this from the side and it was all I could do not to burst out laughing.

Ben's luck wasn't any better in the pit than it was in the Vikings game. He played for a couple hours (I left after a while), but wound up busted out.

You'd think that was the end of the story. You'd be wrong.

We deposited Ben's checks first thing in the morning. Soon after, Bill McHugh got a call from Ben's bank. They weren't going to honor either his cashier's check for $275,000 or the $20,000 personal check.

Well, as you probably know, the purpose of a cashier's check is that it's just like cash. It's the whole basis of paying with a check like that. There's no risk as to the check's viability. Period. For a bank not to honor such a check would have had major implications.

Bill got our attorneys on the phone, who arranged for a judge in Ben's jurisdiction to hold an immediate hearing. While flying to the meeting, our attorneys were discussing the case with the bank's attorneys. Club Cal Neva actually had quite a bit of political clout. I've had former Nevada Senator and Governor Richard Bryan in my office while he was serving in both of those capacities. I had an individual audience with Harry Reid in our boardroom while he was the Senate Minority Leader to discuss an issue vital to our industry. I sat with both of them at dinner as they served in the Senate. I handicapped horses with Governor Bob Miller. I've had dinner and drinks with Mills Lane as he served as Washoe County District Attorney. And that's just me. I was an owner at the Cal Neva, but my joke was I think I owned the paper clips. Trust me, my partners had much more political influence than I even knew about.

By the time our group landed and got to the hearing, Ben's bank decided to come into the hearing and support our side of the argument. This was a much bigger issue than one cashier's check. What Ben was asking went against the core banking laws in America. Had they opposed us and gone with Ben, who just wanted his money back, they'd be opening a huge can of worms of which they wanted no part.

Bill had been updating me back in Reno as things were proceeding. He described the astonished look on Ben's face when he and his attorney came in to the hearing and saw his bankers lining up on our side as "just priceless." I would have loved to see it. Especially after all the shit this guy put me through.

Legally, there isn't much to say. It was a cashier's check; we weren't going to extend Ben, or anyone, $275,000 in credit. We weren't that kind of an operation, just a small casino. He was lucky we went for the $20,000 on his personal check. Meanwhile, Ben pulled most of the money from his account, so we were stuck that last $20,000.

You'd think that was the end of the story. You'd be wrong.

Bill was gone all day, flying back and forth to deal with bankers and lawyers. I talked to him briefly during the Monday night game, so I was updated on everything. We got most of our money and we'd never see Ben again. Too bad. As big of a prick as he was, he was one hell of a customer, an all-time great.

The next day, Tuesday morning, I was polishing up the line for the coming week when Bill came into my office.

"I've got some news," he said to me.

"Yeah? What's up?"

"We're being sued."

"Who's being sued?" I asked.

"Me and you."
"By who?"
"Ben," he said.
"For what?"
"Mental cruelty."
We looked at each other and burst out laughing.

We laughed for 30 to 60 seconds, looked at each other, and cracked up all over again. I don't know how many times, but we simply could not stop. The irony was priceless. This was the cruelest bastard you ever met in your life. Bill and I used to joke about it. Ben was the kind of guy who, had he been born in the Middle Ages, would have had no problem putting someone on the rack. Or flaying him alive. Or having him drawn and quartered in the public square. Or burning him at the stake. Seriously, it didn't take much imagination to see it. This was one cold-blooded son of a bitch.

The lawsuit got dismissed pretty quickly. I never had to give depositions or even talk to an attorney. I guess somewhere in Ben's corner, cooler heads prevailed. Really, it would have been a big joke, but it probably still would have been a pain in the ass for me.

You'd think that would be the end of the story. You'd be wrong.

Bill McHugh was a smart man. He wasn't the easiest guy to get over on. You can only deposit a check twice to be cashed. Since Ben's $20,000 check bounced once, we had only one more shot at it. Bill knew something I sure didn't: one particular day that's the biggest in Ben's industry. Bill held that check for months, finally depositing it on that one big industry day. It cleared. I can only imagine Ben's face when he looked into this account and saw that he was $20,000 short. He would probably call that mental cruelty. Had I been able to see his face, I would have called it hilarious.

Chapter 13

Tell Yolanda *That!*

Every bookmaker has one customer who's a total pain in the ass. Most have more than one, but one guy always stands above the crowd, constantly asking for the most ridiculous things. If it's a big customer, it can present some real problems as it did with Ben, but most of the time, it's a small player who gives the sports book a constant headache. I always wanted to provide the best customer service possible, but sometimes that was impossible.

Early in my career at the Cal Neva, the bane of my existence was Psycho James. "Psycho" was nothing more than a nickname and not meant to be a clinical diagnosis. He was harmless. Actually, he really was a pretty nice guy, but he was missing a few marbles.

He never made a straight bet; it was always a parlay for multiple teams, never just a two-teamer. And with every bet, it was something with James. If he won an early game or two, I heard, "Chris, Chris, can I void the rest of the parlay and get my winnings now?"

I told him, "No, James, you can't do that."

Or it was, "Chris, Chris, I have over on my ticket, can I switch it to under?"

"No, James, you can't do that."

Every conversation really did start with him saying my name at least twice, and usually a lot more than that—part of that whole "Psycho" thing.

My second in command at that time was Yolanda Acuna.

Yolanda has had a long and very successful career in the sports book industry in Nevada. After she left Cal Neva, she worked at Caesars Palace and the Hilton under my cousin Art Manteris, then at the Mirage for Jimmy Vaccaro. Though she was often in the background, the bosses relied on her to get things done. It was no different when she worked with me. The Cal Neva's race and sport books were in two different rooms, and while I was almost always on the sports side, Yolanda was mostly in the race book where she oversaw all the administrative functions of the operation.

I got tired of dealing with Psycho James on a daily basis, so I started blaming everything on Yolanda. "James, I'd love to change your parlay from Red Sox to Yankees, but Yolanda says I can't do that." Or, "James, I'd be happy to void your eight-teamer and pay you for a two-teamer, but Yolanda would kill me if I did."

"Chris, Chris, so Yolanda is the big boss, huh, Chris?"

"Yep, James. Yolanda is the big boss."

And that was only a partial falsehood. Yolanda did run the back room and if I did try to accommodate some, or even one, of James' crazy requests, she probably *would have* killed me.

Once I had James convinced that Yolanda ruled the roost, he was absolutely petrified of her. He wore hoodies long before they became fashionable. When Yolanda walked through the sports book, James shrank down in his seat and tightened the strings of his hoodie until the opening was no bigger than enough to give him some tunnel vision and allow in enough air to breathe. Of course, she had no idea any of this was even going on. James was totally off her radar; she didn't even know who he was. The guys in the sports book could see James' Yolandaphobia and thought it was hilarious. When she walked back out of the sports book, everyone could see James breathe a sigh of relief, like he'd just escaped the gallows.

This was the early '80s. Few college basketball games were televised, but the Big East started broadcasting its games regularly.

One Saturday, games were being played all day. James had put in his usual $5 8-team parlay starting with some early games, going through the mid-afternoon, and ending with Syracuse, the only televised game that evening.

James swept the board on his early games and I could see he was getting nervous. He won all the early-afternoon games, too. So now he was sitting on seven winners on his 8-teamer. He had about two hours until the Syracuse game tipped off. If he won that game, his $5 bet would pay $1,000.

"Chris, Chris, Chris, can I void the Syracuse game and just get paid for a seven-teamer?"

"Sorry, James, I can't do that."

"You would if Yolanda let you though, right, Chris?"

"Oh, yeah, James. I'd do it in a heartbeat, but Yolanda'd be all over me."

"I know that, Chris, I know that. But you can't get in trouble with Yolanda, right, Chris?"

"Yep, James. You got it."

James was going around to everyone in the book to see if he could get anyone to stake him some money to hedge his bet on Syracuse. *He* might have been nuts, but no one else in the book was crazy enough to lend him any money.

Besides, the number moved against him. James had Syracuse -6.5 on the parlay and the game went down to Syracuse -5. So if he did bet the other side, he could only take +5. If Syracuse won by 6, he'd lose both his original parlay and the hedge bet. No one was going to take that risk. Certainly not for Psycho James. He had no choice but to root for Syracuse and hope for the best.

Syracuse was just beginning to emerge as one of the nation's top college basketball powerhouses. They coasted to a 10-point lead at the end of the first half. James was pacing in anguish like an expectant father in a 1940s' black-and-white movie. The thousand-dollar payoff was right within his grasp and he could taste it.

The second half tipped off and Syracuse began to extend

their lead. They went up by 14, then 17, then 20, and poured it on from there. With about five minutes to play, they were up by 30 and James couldn't lose. He was feeling it now. James pulled out his ticket and ran to the counter right where I was standing and flashed it to me like an Apache warrior showing off his latest scalp.

"Chris, Chris, Chris, look here. I beat you out of a thousand dollars. That's right, Chris, a thousand dollars! Tell Yolanda *that*! Whoooooo!"

James held his ticket up for the world to see. He had a rolled-up newspaper in his other hand and started galloping around the sports book like a horse, whipping himself in the ass with the paper, all the while still brandishing his ticket. "Tell Yolanda *that*! Tell Yolanda *that*!" he shouted. "That's right, Chris. A thousand dollars! Tell Yolanda *that*!" I'm sure it was the biggest score of his life. Not only that, he got to stick it to the man. Or in this case, the woman.

Behind the counter, we were holding our stomachs in laughter—when who should come walking into the sports book but the Big Boss herself? She saw the whole staff in stitches and some nut running around like a horse getting whipped in mid-stretch and screaming her name. She glanced over at me with a look that said, "What the hell is going on?"

I had to spill the beans on myself and tell her the whole story. She was slightly mad, but she had to laugh as James continued his victory laps, all the while chanting, "Tell Yolanda *that*! Tell Yolanda *that*!"

James collected his winnings and went from $5 parlays to $100 parlays. Needless to say, the thousand was gone in a few days.

But "Tell Yolanda *that*!" lives on. I call or see Yolanda every so often and every time I greet her with, "Tell Yolanda *that*!" and we both start laughing.

I have no idea if James is dead or alive. I hope he's all right, wherever he might be.

Chapter 14

My Biggest Asshole

Psycho James might have been my biggest pain in the ass, but he really was a harmless soul and he gave us a story and an image we've laughed about for more than 30 years and counting. Another customer gave new meaning to the word "asshole."

It was in early 1991 that I became an owner at the Cal Neva. Being a sub-S, it was a closed corporation. The shares weren't traded in the open market in any way. People like me essentially had to be invited to become a stockholder. After putting in 10 years with the company, they allowed me to buy in. The stock wasn't given to me. There were some favorable terms attached, but I paid real money to acquire it.

Through the years, I'd also set it up so my salary was only a portion of my compensation. In a good year, my salary amounted to about one-third of my actual pay. The other two-thirds came to me in performance bonuses. I wouldn't even count my dividends. I used those to pay off my debt to the company for the stock.

My reasons for doing this were twofold. One, I believed in my ability to run the business and maximize the profit in my department. Two, I wanted the structure of my pay to be such that if I took a bet, it would have more of an effect on me personally than anyone else in the company.

That's not to say I had a bigger cut than anyone else. It did mean that it put the onus on me, so if I wanted to take a bet, we took it. No one overruled me on anything concerning the action we took. I didn't have someone from upstairs come down and tell me to put up a higher number on the favorite on some game or not to put this guy or that on for so much money. None of that. At the Cal Neva, as far as taking action in the sports book, I was the boss. Start to finish.

Every business, every businessman, every everyone has that one person they have to deal with who just makes them cringe every time. Even the thought of that one person can give you shivers or disgust or outright anger. I had one such guy. And in a business renowned for its sheer number of assholes, this one guy overshadowed them all.

This customer, "Bobby," was from the Bay Area. I never got his whole story, but I think he was involved in the tech industry. He definitely had a lot of money. I have a feeling he came from money, but also made a lot on his own. My guess was he fronted venture capital for some startups, some of which made a fortune.

Cal Neva was a small company, but we took decent-sized bets. In the early '90s, our college football limit was $3,000 and we took $10,000 in the NFL. These limits were for anyone who walked up to the counter. Whether they were wiseguys or squares, regular customers or newcomers, everyone got at least that much on a bet. Once we established a relationship with someone, we could, would, and often did take a lot more. We weren't Caesars Palace or the Mirage, but we booked some major action.

Bobby always wanted more than the limit on every bet he made. He was no wiseguy, but neither was he a square. He never took the worst of a number, he never played in the pit, and his wife never played the slots at the Cal Neva. They were doing both across the street where they were full RF&B (room, food and beverage) at Harrah's. To make it short, he wasn't the kind of guy for whom I extended the limits.

His m.o. was to try to put you in a position where he could question your manhood, usually over not taking a bet as big as he wanted to make. Meanwhile, those assholes at Harrah's weren't exactly taking all his action either, even though he was giving them every bit of his square play in the casino. He regaled me with stories about how Jimmy Vaccaro took the kind of action he was looking for at the Mirage and how Caesars put him on for some big numbers. I told him to take a look around at our humble little joint and asked him if it in any way, shape, or form resembled the Mirage.

Bobby loved betting totals. We only took $500 on college football totals and $1,000 on NFL totals. We took lower limits on totals, just like everyone else, because we didn't do as well on totals, just like everyone else. So Bobby started betting round robins with sides to totals, then want to come back and bet them straight. Or he would say he was betting the side and the total for the same amount and ask what I'd take? I informed him of the limit on the total and if that was his decision, he could take the lower of the two limits. He always, and I mean *always*, made a huge scene to try to make me look like a douchebag, but I didn't take the bait. Fuck him. I was still putting him on for more than anyone in town. He didn't have other options—unless he went to Las Vegas.

Then one day … on a Friday evening with a full slate of college football the next day, he sauntered his fat arrogant ass up to the counter and said to me, "You're supposed to be some hotshot bookmaker, right? Let's see if you have any balls."

I didn't flinch. I knew his act all too well by now.

"I have one college game I want to bet for thirty thousand," he continued. "But you can't make any phone calls to check with your boss, or go and check any lines, or anything like that. You just have to take the bet. If you step away from the counter, the deal is off. Now let's see what you've got, Mr. Bigshot."

Back then we didn't have access to immediate information like everyone does today. I knew I could easily be sitting on a stale number. Also, being a Friday night, someone could have gotten hurt or suspended and I had yet to find out about it. That was all possible. He also had no idea I could take any bet I wanted without any repercussions from anyone.

"I'll tell you what," I said. "You might know more than I do about a certain game, I admit that. So I don't want to take one bet for thirty thousand. But here's what I will do. I'll take three bets for thirty thousand each. And the same deal goes for you. You can't make any phone calls to check any other lines. You can't check with your wife to make sure it's okay for you to bet the ninety. All you can do is step back, take a look at the board, and pick your three games. If you leave for any reason, the deal's off. So tell me what three games you want."

"I don't want to bet three games for that much. I only want one."

"Well, I don't want one for that much, but I don't mind taking three."

"I'm not going to do that."

"Look," I said, "let's say your one game is a sure winner. Okay, I'll give you that. All you have to do is split the other two, you'll lose three thousand in juice money and you got me for twenty-seven thousand."

"I don't have three games."

"Flip a coin. Throw a dart. All you have to do is split the two games and you nail me for twenty-seven."

"I don't have ninety-nine on me."

"I know you can get a marker for as much as you want across the street. Just give me the games. I'll write the tickets for you and hold them until you get back."

"I'm not going to do that."

"Well, I'm not going to take the one. The limit is three thousand. Fire away."

He walked out with his tail between his legs and didn't bet a thing. After that, he still came in, but never asked for more than the limit and never made a scene.

Making him bet three games was a bit of an improvisation I'd learned from listening to Jackie Gaughan and Warren Nelson tell stories about the old days running real gambling joints. When some hotshot player came in to their casinos and asked what the limit was at the tables, they told him, "Whatever your first bet is, that's the limit."

Those old bastards were plenty goddamn sharp. And I guarantee both of those guys would take a bet. You just weren't going to cherry pick them with their own money. You had to beat them with yours. Even though this wasn't a direct correlation, I knew booking three bets would give me a hell of a lot better chance than just one.

By the way, forget what I said earlier. Thanks to Uncle Jack and Roxy, not many guys were getting information quicker than I was. So even though I told him his first bet was probably a lock, I was lying. There was a better chance of him going 0-3 than 3-0.

I'm pretty sure Bobby started taking most of his action to Las Vegas. Years later, I was visiting John Falenski in one of the books he was running and I saw Bobby. "Is that …?"

Before I could even finish, Johnny said, "Do you know that motherfucker? I hate him."

I had to laugh. At least I knew it wasn't personal. He was a huge asshole to everyone.

Chapter 15

My Run-in with the FBI

When Cal Neva increased the parlay-card odds, our business exploded. Within a matter of weeks, we were suddenly dominating the action in northern Nevada. It was a boon so big, none of us had come close to anticipating it.

That next spring, the United States Football League started up. For those of you too young to remember, it was a spring football league. Some USFL players (Steve Young, Jim Kelly, Reggie White) went on to Hall of Fame careers in the NFL. The failure of that league is one of the greatest travesties in the history of American sports. Why? Primarily, Donald Trump, who owned the New Jersey Generals, had visions of making it into something it was never meant to be. It was yet another venture he bankrupted without taking responsibility. Don't get me started.

The USFL ran for three seasons. The football itself was pretty good and the betting action on an extra season was fantastic. I mentioned once during a management meeting that it wouldn't be that hard to run parlay cards virtually year-round. Between the NFL and USFL, with their regular seasons and playoffs, there would be only a couple weeks with no football action. I could piece something together during that off-time with baseball, basketball, or hockey. Plus, "Parlay Cards 52 Weeks A Year!" would be a great advertising slogan for us. We were already leading the whole state in parlay-card action and this would give us even more separation.

Warren Nelson loved the idea. Warren had an affinity for the little guys who came in to gamble with their modest bank-rolls and he had a vision of turning that market into a fortune. Sure, the big players were nice, but Cal Neva was built on the player two or three steps from being a bust-out. And once they did bust out, Warren gave them a chance to get back on their feet. Parlay-card bettors were Warren's kind of player—smart enough to know sports and willing to take a shot to make a score.

Once the USFL folded (fucking Trump), I assumed we would shit-can the Parlay Cards 52 Weeks A Year. Wrong. Warren wouldn't hear of it. He still liked the idea enough to keep it around. I put together a generic baseball card to carry us through the summer, but the odds were much shorter than for football cards, which had escalated our business. That wasn't making Warren very happy.

I'd put out some basketball games in the brief period with the USFL still happening when there was no football. Warren not only wanted to offer them for the whole NBA season, but also with those great payout prices.

This was a bad idea.

First, we didn't subscribe to a ties-lose policy like a lot of others in the industry. We had everything on the half-point, so there were no ties at all. That was part of the strategy that elevated our business to the top. I knew Warren wouldn't want to change that; I didn't either. What I did want to change were the payouts. Putting out a line on Wednesday for the weekend's football games on parlay cards wasn't too tough. But to put out a basketball line on Wednesday for the weekend's games is crazy. The basketball numbers moved a ton on Saturday and Sunday mornings. So, putting out a line the day of the game was tough enough.

My concerns, however, fell on deaf ears. That's what Warren wanted and that's what was going to happen. Period.

I was personally betting the college hoops fairly heavily at this point, so I was as up on the numbers as anyone. I knew how dangerous it was to allow guys to bet into early numbers that I had to lock in on a parlay card. It wasn't even bookmaking; with a parlay card there were no numbers to move. Once the cards got into bettors' hands, all I could do was manage the risk.

To solidify my numbers, I asked Uncle Jack and Scott Kaminsky to help me. Scott was the main basketball handicapper working at Roxy Roxborough's Las Vegas Sports Consultants. I gave them a list of the games I was interested in (any with marquee teams or that were televised) and if we were all in relative agreement, I put them on the card. Almost exclusively, they were college games. The NBA was too volatile. With teams playing four times a week, too many injuries and situations compromised an advance number. At least the colleges had only one game in between, so there wasn't nearly the opportunity to have something unexpected happen.

Warren also wouldn't allow me to take a game off the card unless there was an injury. I really shouldn't blame Warren for that. I hated doing it, too. If we were off on a number, we were going to gamble with it.

Warren did let me make one adjustment: set the minimum number of teams to play on the card at four, rather than the three that was the minimum on the football card.

I have to tell you, even though I disagreed with Warren on this one issue (and a few others over the years), he was a dream to work for. I never *never* NEVER got heat from Warren for losing. He knew my numbers were solid and he had faith in me as a bookmaker. We had some big losses at times, believe me, but I never got called on the carpet for them. I might hear it from some of the other partners, but never from Warren Nelson. Man, I was spoiled.

Just so you know, here's my parlay-card paytable. If you

know parlay betting, you can see it's very playable for a serious handicapper.

Teams			Pays		
3	for	3	6.75	for	1
4	for	4	13	for	1
5	for	5	26	for	1
6	for	6	54	for	1
7	for	7	104	for	1
8	for	8	208	for	1
9	for	9	420	for	1
10	for	10	850	for	1
11	for	11	1,600	for	1
12	for	12	3,000	for	1
13	for	13	6,000	for	1
14	for	14	12,000	for	1
15	for	15	25,000	for	1

Those are the football odds. In basketball, I eliminated the 3-teamers and anything more than 10-teamers. But ask any pro bettor and he'll tell you—if you can play into a locked-in line on Wednesday for a college basketball game on Saturday, it can easily be worth taking a shot.

So I hated this card. I hated booking it. I hated managing it. I hated making the line on Wednesday for Saturday and Sunday games. I hated everything about it, with all my heart. We did, somehow, make a little money with it. Not much, and certainly not enough to justify the effort that went into it. Tough shit. None of that mattered. Warren wanted it and we were using it.

Then one day … Warren got a call from Cal Neva's head of security. It seems an informant for the FBI had accused me of purposely putting bad numbers on the parlay card, so Uncle Jack and I could bet into them.

Oh yeah?

Stale Numbers

The parlay-card reference to "locked-in lines" comes from the fact that a line can't be changed once it's printed on the card. Hence, if something happens between printing and game time—an injury, a trade, anything that causes a big line movement—the bettor can bet the "stale" line that remains on the card and is better than the market price. It's a strategy that's used by parlay-card bettors and contest players.

I've mentioned that the little old Club Cal Neva was surprisingly well-connected politically. Part of that connection was with local law enforcement, including the Reno office of the FBI.

Warren came and told me about the feds' suspicion. I don't think he even asked me if it was true. First of all, I think he understood me enough to know I would never do such a thing. It would never even occur to me. Secondly, the card was for the whole world to bet on, not just Uncle Jack and me. Third, I'd been trying to convince him from Day One that booking this card was a terrible idea.

Warren probably wasn't supposed to tell me, but he let me know who the informant was. It was a ticket writer at one of the local sports books who'd been nailed in some bookmaking charge back east and was working for the FBI under a witness-protection plan. In case you aren't aware, once you turn informant, they don't exactly set you up in Buckingham Palace. You still have to earn a living. Also, if you want to stay in their good graces, you have to keep delivering information to them. If you don't have anything real, you damn well better make something up; otherwise, your usefulness runs out. This prick tried to extend his utility at my expense.

I knew this guy from going into his sports book and betting.

He had noticeably shifty eyes. Still, I never suspected he was an informant. I just thought he was a fucking weasel. How complete a fucking weasel, I soon found out. He'd been an informant in Las Vegas for a year or so. He had a different name there, but a guy recognized him when he came up to work in Reno and called himself Frank. When I told Uncle Jack, he blew his stack. He was absolutely livid. He was working now for Michael Gaughan and he didn't need more trumped-up bullshit from the FBI. He told me he was flying up to Reno the next day. He wanted to get a look at this guy.

I think I've made it pretty clear, Uncle Jack doesn't take shit from anyone. He's not a big man physically, but he *is* intimidating. I picked him up at the airport and he wasted no time. We went straight to Frank's sports book.

We walked in and there was Frank, behind the counter writing tickets. Uncle Jack went up to his window and stood right in front of the guy. Frank looked up, saw him, and started shaking. His eyes were shifting right, left, back and forth, desperately searching for a way out. He'd lied about Uncle Jack and me and now he was caught in that lie.

Uncle Jack isn't violent, but Frank didn't know that. Of course, it was lucky for him; otherwise, he wouldn't have made it home from work that night without one of his FBI buddies escorting him.

Uncle Jack continued to stand in front of Frank for about a minute. A minute, under those circumstances, is a very long time. Count to 60 and imagine having to sit there while a guy you're afraid of and just lied about is there giving you a death stare.

Theo finally turned to me and said, "I don't know this fuckin' guy. Let's go."

We went to the Cal Neva. Uncle Jack wanted to see Warren. I don't think Warren needed any explanations, but Uncle Jack wanted to tell him how ridiculous an accusation like that was.

Warren knew that, but I think he still appreciated someone like Uncle Jack coming to him. There was a great mutual respect between the two of them. They really were two of the great and influential men in my life.

The head of security was another story. A former cop, those guys don't believe *anything*. That I was from Pittsburgh made it worse. A lot of people who've lived out west their whole lives are suspicious of anyone from back east. Add to the fact that I was a bookmaker, from a bookmaking family, and spent time in Las Vegas. No way this guy was believing that I was on the up-and-up. He'd always cast a wary eye my way and this little episode as good as proved his suspicions to him.

A few years later, I was hanging out in a bar where long-time Renoites, including cops, liked to drink. A guy came up and introduced himself as the head of the local FBI office. Our conversation quickly turned to the episode with the basketball parlay cards. He told me he knew the informant was full of shit. Really, anyone with half a brain would realize the guy was lying. He never said, but I think that's why he went to Cal Neva security rather than conduct a real investigation. I'm fortunate Warren had enough common sense to realize how ludicrous the whole thing was. My life could have changed on a different decision by him. Any number of business executives (most of them wearing suits and having a college degree) would think it was just easier to get rid of someone like me and not have to worry about it anymore.

One good thing did come of it. Once Warren saw that the numbers were so bad, even though we were trying our best to put out good numbers, he finally let me shit-can the card. I don't like how we arrived at that final solution, but in the long run, it was no harm no foul for me personally.

As far as Frank goes, he disappeared shortly after. I guess the FBI had to move him to a place where no one would know him. I have to think karma catches up with a guy like that. If he crossed the wrong guy, he's either buried in the desert somewhere or in a lead-weighted duffle bag at the bottom of some lake or ocean. I can't say I'd be sorry.

Chapter 16

The World Champion of Race Horse Handicapping

When I talk about my career at Cal Neva, I tell people I started in 1981 and left in 2003. That's partly true. The whole truth is I left on January 1, 1989. They asked me to come back in August of that same year. And I did.

I was burned out. I had a few problems with Bill McHugh, the boss, and Jeff Siri, second in command. When I returned, we patched up our differences and we remain friends to this day. The contentions that split us briefly are water under the bridge. However, at one time, things weren't all that rosy between me and those two.

In 1982, Warren Nelson came up with the idea for a horseracing contest. Although there are an abundance of them now, this was the very first. Since it was the first and only such contest at the time, we dubbed it the World Championship of Race Horse Handicapping. It's one more thing we started at Cal Neva that will probably be lost to the gaming historians, but I'm proud to say we kicked it all off.

The format was simple. The buy-in was $500. We chose a few of the major tracks and you had to bet 10% of your bankroll on 10 races each day over a four-day period.

The first day, everyone bet $50 a race (win, place, and show only). At the end of the day, the bankrolls were adjusted according to your win or loss. The next day, you bet 10% of the new bankroll on 10 races. For example, if you doubled your bankroll to $1,000 on the first day, you bet $100 per race. But if you lost $300, your bankroll was now $200 and you bet $20 a race. If you lost the whole buy-in, you were out of the contest. The same went for days three and four. If you had a big lead, you couldn't just sit on it. Your whole bankroll had to be in action every day.

For prize money, we guaranteed $50,000 to be split among the top five finishers. However, you also got to keep whatever money you had left over from your bankroll. So the prize money was significantly higher than the $50,000 we advertised. It really was the best contest format a race book ever came up with.

Unfortunately, contests came in after us and boasted big guaranteed prize money, because they kept the entire buy-in. No surprise, the general public couldn't figure out that our contest gave them a much bigger bang for their buck and eventually it died out. (I refer you back to the chapter titled "H.L. Mencken Was Right.")

The contest was still going strong in the summer of 1989 during the time that I'd left the Cal Neva. I resigned on December 31, 1988, so I was eligible to enter the contest in June 1989. A lot of people still weren't aware that I'd left and they were a little surprised to see me among the contestants. They were probably even more surprised to see my name up with the leaders from Day One.

I nailed three to four winners in each of the first three days of the contest, all for decent prices. As we entered the fourth and final day, I started the day in third place.

I had my eye on one horse in particular the whole day. He was in the last race at Bay Meadows, a stakes race for which Robbie Black, a pretty good rider from southern California, had traveled north to mount this horse. He looked live, but I thought his morning-line price of 9/2 was probably reasonably close to where he'd go off. I also believed another horse in that race would go off at close to even money. He was ridden by one of the good northern California riders who never got the credit their southern brethren enjoyed.

As the day progressed, I pulled in a couple of nice winners. I knew I had to be in contention for the top prize, but I wasn't sure how close. Everything was being held pretty close to the vest by the other players and the folks at Cal Neva running the contest.

All those years that I ran the contest, I made the first prize $35,000 and second $10,000. I kept first and second at such a wide difference because I wanted players to go for the gusto and, of course, it gave me, the bookmaker, a better chance at beating them. Now I was caught by rules that I'd established, a spider tangled in his own web. I had to go for the extra $25,000 gusto, too.

The last race at Bay Meadows wound up being the last race of the last day of the contest. When the odds opened, the horse I had wanted to bet all day, ridden by Robbie Black, had been bet down from 9/2 to even money. Everyone was looking at the same things I was. If I bet the horse at even money, even if he won, I might not have had enough to win the contest. I had to make a quick switch.

Switching sides is always a dangerous move for a gambler. I like to trust my first instincts. But what choice did I have? Sticking with my original selection, I had to hope he won, plus hope the other contestants were playing the wrong side of the strategy game. Or I could try to beat him.

I tried to beat him.

The horse I'd originally thought would go off at even money, the one to beat, was completely overlooked in the betting and was going off at 7/2, an unbelievable overlay. I saw a ton of value in the choice and even though I had planned all day on beating him, I was now betting on him.

Turning for home, Robbie Black took his horse out to a length lead with a cavalry charge chasing him. My horse was wide around the turn, but closing steadily in the middle of the turf course.

The last jump before the wire, my horse got up to win it by a head.

I felt unbelievably lucky switching to the winner. Any gambler knows that doesn't happen all too often. I had a pretty decent amount in my bankroll. I had to hope it could hold up.

I could look inside a Plexiglas window to where my old office was in the sports book. Sitting there were Bill McHugh and Jeff Siri, along with the auditing staff, running a report to see the results. I knew most of the guys who were in contention and started asking about what they finished with. There was no sense hiding it now. Whatever they had, they had. I couldn't find anyone with a bigger bankroll than mine. I thought I had everyone covered, but I couldn't be sure.

The auditors would tell us who the winner was.

I kept looking up into my old office to see everyone's reactions. I knew the last thing they wanted to see was me winning this thing. It would be like your ex-wife marrying a billionaire or a guy known for his huge wang. I tried to be patient; I knew the longer they were up there, the better chance I had. If I came up the winner the first time they ran the program, they'd surely run it again. And again. That looked like exactly what they were doing.

My wife had come down earlier when I told her I was in serious contention to win this thing. She was a little more schooled now in the nuances of gamblers.

While I was watching the goings-on in the office, I spotted the marketing manager, Charmaine LeMay. With sports such a big part of our business at Cal Neva, Charmaine and I worked pretty closely together on a lot of marketing projects and had become pretty good friends.

Eventually, I saw Bill throw his hands in the air in an exasperated gesture that I read as, "Fuck it. Let's get it over with." Everyone gathered their materials and made their way to the podium for the awards ceremony.

There was a short flight of stairs from the sports book office to the main floor. I had a hunch to keep my eyes on Charmaine. She'd be making the presentation to the winners, so she had the list of who placed where. As she made her way down the steps, I could see her looking around. I was hoping it was me she was looking for. We made eye contact and she quickly looked away trying to hide a big smile on her face.

"I won," I told my wife.

"Don't say that. You're going to jinx it!"

I told you she had picked up a lot in those couple years.

"No," I said. "You can forget about it. It's all over. I won."

"No! No!" she was pleading with me. "Don't say it!"

"Trust me. It's over. I won."

Of course, I was right. The second Charmaine smiled, I knew I had it in the bag. Bill and Jeff weren't too happy, but what can I say? I played and won. They didn't stick around for the awards ceremony; instead, they went across the street and had a few cocktails. They suffered some pain that day, due to my pleasure, a symmetrical and ironic yin and yang between their feelings and mine. That's the way it goes sometimes.

I was playing all my selections in the regular race book, too. I had some nice exactas and quinellas to go along with my win bets. With the $35,000 in prize money, plus what remained in my bankroll and what I made in the book, I came away with about $50,000 for the four days of handicapping.

A few months later, Bill convinced me to come back to the Cal Neva. As I said before, any differences we had were resolved and I eventually became a partner in the company. Bill admitted that when I won the contest, it helped convince him to make an effort to get me back in the fold.

Somewhere in my junk, I still have the wall board from that race. Next time I go through all my shit, I'll look for that sheet and try to remember the horse's name. I'll probably forget again soon after. But I'll never forget that win. That was a nice one.

Chapter 17

A Day at the Races

The Cal Neva contest story had a happy ending. The other horse racing story that stands out in my life was, well, a little different.

When I moved to Las Vegas, I had a little experience betting horses, but none to speak of in handicapping them.

When I worked at the Stardust, a few guys showed me how to read the *Daily Racing Form* and gave me pointers on what to look for. I started playing a little and I got pretty good. I hit the 1980 Kentucky Derby with a bet on Genuine Risk, a filly beating the boys for the first time in years. I also hit the Belmont with Temperence Hill, going off at 50/1.

Needless to say, I was hooked after that. I started playing pretty heavily and doing pretty well.

For whatever reason, handicapping horses appeals to the way my brain works. I really can't explain it any better than that. But I've had a lot of success betting horses and at 62 years old, I'm still way ahead of the game. Not many can say that.

When I started booking horses at the race book, it was before pari-mutuel pools could be bet into in Nevada. So all the money went into, or out of, our pocket, as the case might be. When guys came in to bet, I tried to pick their brains. I could see that trainers, jockeys, and owners all had their own angles. Most stuck with the same one over and over and picking up on them was a good way to build a bankroll.

Early in my career at Cal Neva, I became friends with Fred, who'd owned horses and still bred some. He was living just outside the Bay Area at the time. At the tracks, he knew the grooms, starters, jockeys, trainers, owners, and even guys in management. He read the *Form*, but any serious plays he made were from an angle he picked up or inside information guys like him seem to get. Fred was about 25 years older than I was and like a lot of people in this racket, he was as gruff as could be, but had a real heart of gold.

Fred moved horse bets for some of his connections who didn't want to put the money into the pari-mutuel pools. He booked some of the action himself and laid some off with me at the Cal Neva. Booking horses American-style sucked, to put it directly. We paid what the track paid, so there was no book-making, no moving a number to try to attract money the other way. All you could do was figure out the extensions (the amount the book is willing to lose on any one particular bet or race) you were willing to gamble with and enforce your limits. That was it. But Cal Neva always did pretty well booking the horses—as a matter of fact, better than other race books in Nevada.

I had given Fred my parameters as to what he could bet and even though he was the kind of wiseguy 90% of Nevada bookmakers tossed out of their joints, he was a good customer and a good friend. I try to tell the suit-and-tie bookmakers it's good to make friends with the wiseguys and they look at me like I'm talking to them in Greek.

A benefit of my friendship with Fred was he would tell me what he was doing—after he made his bets, of course. If he had something really good or if he was just laying off a piece of his action to me, he let me know. Fred also got me down on horses he was playing if I didn't have time to run across the street or if he was out of town and had something especially good. We weren't partners, but we definitely had a good working relationship.

Then one day ... Fred called me in Reno. It was after dinner.

"Can you make it down here tomorrow?" he asked. "I think we might have something." Fred was at the now-defunct Bay Meadows in San Mateo, California.

Well, that was all I needed to hear. "Yeah, count me in. Now what is it we've got going?"

"There's a half-million-dollar carryover in the pick six and the kids think we might have a shot to take it down."

"The kids" were two guys, a little younger than I was, who had been supplying us with terrific information. They worked for one of the leading northern California trainers. Like a lot of businesses, the underlings know more about what's going on than the boss. One thing Fred told them, and something I learned from him, was, "Don't tell me who *can* win. Tell me who *can't* win."

They'd told Fred that almost every favorite in the pick six was lame, sore, or coming off a race where he was juiced up (running on some sort of medication, usually illegal). While those horses with no chance of winning would chew up money in the betting pool, we'd have a chance to take a big chunk of it with live horses that really could win. We were looking to put together as big a ticket as we could, to cover as many options as possible. Fred had a couple other guys lined up and we were all getting together at a restaurant in San Mateo at 11 the next morning.

This was late summer 1984. My oldest son had been born earlier that summer, but I remember the date for another reason entirely. I packed up the wife and kid and off we went, over Donner Summit, down the west slope of the Sierra, and into the Bay Area to meet Fred and his friends in San Mateo. My in-laws lived in Fremont, so they were coming to the restaurant as well. Then my wife and infant son would spend the day with Grandma. My father-in-law was a horseplayer and he wanted in on the action. That was good with Fred; the bigger ticket we could put in the better.

We went through the program and I have to say, it was shocking how many short-priced favorites these guys told us had absolutely no shot of winning. We were all decent handicappers, so we picked horses that had the best chances once the major contenders were eliminated. After making our picks and cutting down the ticket as much as we could, the kids pointed out that the one favorite they did like was in the last race of the day. He was 7/5 on the morning line and the only horse in the race with a chance.

So we singled him on our ticket. We figured if we were alive going into the last, we'd try to come up with something from there. As it was, our ticket was about $10,000. I put in a little over $1,000, which was a monster bet for a 28-year-old young father. But I knew this was a good shot to make some serious dough.

The track was jammed for a weekday. We played around the first few races and made a few bucks. Between my own handicapping skills and the bunch of old warhorses who really knew the racket, we came up with some good stuff early. It was shaping up to be a nice day.

A $30 horse took the first race of the pick six and we had it. Probably 90% of the other tickets were dead going into race two, but we were alive. Not only that, but I had an exacta with the winner, too.

In the second race, a $20 horse won. We had him. I didn't know how many pick six tickets could have been alive, but ours was one of them.

Ten-dollar horses won the third and fourth and we had both. I was also having a huge day betting the races individually, besides the pick six ticket.

My wife, mother-in-law, and two-month-old son met us at the track. My wife was still pretty green, but my mother-in-law, married to a horseplayer like my father-in-law, was hip to what was going on.

In the fifth race, another $20 horse took first. We had him

too. We were looking at five winners in five races and not one of them paid in the single digits.

Back in those days, they didn't post any info about who was live and what it would pay; you were pretty much shooting in the dark. Fortunately, Fred knew people in management. He called into the office and heard that the payoff was over $750,000. There was one live ticket. Ours.

My cut, including the consolation tickets we already had wrapped up, was going to be close to $100,000, so my heart was pumping pretty good. Hell, it's pumping pretty good now as I write this and I know what happens.

We now needed a 7/5 shot to win the last race. We put money on all the other horses in the race to make sure we would at least get a little something extra in our pocket. Fred had paddock privileges, so we bet $500 to win on our horse, then he and I went into the saddling area. Just as the announcer said, "Jockey's up," we handed the $500 ticket to our jockey. He took it, looked at it, gave a nod of appreciation, and mounted our $750,000 horse.

It was the kind of race you no longer see in North America. It was even pretty rare back in 1984. It was a mile and a quarter on the main track, Kentucky Derby distance, run by some of the cheapest horses on the grounds. I was, actually, joking when I said that it was our $750,000 horse. Actually, they were all four-year-old or more with a claiming price of $7,500. Yep. Complete garbage. Add two zeroes to those glue-factory candidates and you'll get to what the race was worth to us.

We were all up in the Turf Club, my wife and I and the bunch of old-time rounders.

The horses went into the gate and none of us could say a word.

It was a hot day. I had some serious saddlebags under my armpits. I can't imagine that the others didn't.

They opened the gate and the jock took our horse right to the front. He went the first quarter in about 23 flat, covering the half in 47 and change. For those of you who might not be familiar with the horseracing game, that's really fast. Actually, it's way too fast for some future can of Alpo to sustain that speed for a mile and a quarter. If you wondered why I remember it was 1984, let me tell you. I had Swale in all the Triple Crown races. He won the Derby and Belmont, which gave me my stake for the action on the pick six. He also won them pretty much on the front end, but running slower fractions than our bottom-of-the-rung claimer.

I leaned over to Fred, whose face was already white as bone china, and said, "He's got fractions faster than Swale."

God rest his soul, Swale was about a $20 million horse before he passed away tragically, and this was a $7,500 piece of shit. We were dead and we knew it.

Even though our horse was about seven lengths out in front, we both slumped back in our chairs. You could see that the other guys with us also knew exactly what was going to happen.

Not my wife. (Ex-wife now. Not because of this. We had a million other problems.) She was standing up and cheering, screaming her lungs out. She looked at me and I know she said something, but I can't remember what. She was either mad at me for being so doom-and-gloom (probably) or pissed because I was playing it cool while we were about to make a big score (maybe, but I could never have been that cool, and even she was smart enough to know it).

My mind is a bit of a blur from here, so I don't remember the rest of the fractions, but our horse hit the top of the lane about 10 lengths in front.

Don't forget, all the other horses in the race were even bigger pieces of shit than ours. After all, he was 7/5 over the field. He had a big enough lead now, where I was thinking, maybe … possibly …

Then he started shortening stride like a defensive lineman nearing the goal line trying to run back a 100-yard fumble return.

We were getting close to the finish and one horse was coming. This wasn't exactly Silky Sullivan or Secretariat or even a decent allowance horse. Nonetheless, he was gaining with every jump. At the 16th pole we still led by about two.

Fred and I, against our better judgment, stood up and started rooting for our horse. The other garbage in the race gave us a chance. We were praying for the wire to magically vault forward. Only a few yards would do it.

It wasn't to be. Our horse got nailed at the wire by about a head. We led for just short of a mile and a quarter, but we needed one less jump to the wire and three quarters of a million would have been ours.

Well, we all went for it again the following day, but we didn't have the same vulnerable favorites. We didn't hit that next day, but a bunch of people did. I wound up making a little money over the two days, but it was a perfect storm the first day and we just couldn't quite pull it off.

Fred and I have lamented over giving that goddamned jockey that $500 win ticket for 30-some years since. The guy wasn't exactly Bill Shoemaker. He got so excited, he forgot he was riding a cheap horse in a mile and a quarter race, like an over-excited teenager trying to get laid for the first time.

I've still made some nice scores on the horses, but that one would have been beyond nice. Oh well. The ex-wife probably would have wound up with most of it anyway.

Chapter 18

Dingo Food

By 2002, I was starting to get pretty frustrated at Cal Neva. We'd gone through a new CEO who took us in a bad direction. I could sense some of the older stockholders were ready to abandon ship. Plus, the property needed some serious reinvestment.

The sports book was doing fine and I was getting paid well. However, the Cal Neva was more like a sports book that had a casino than a casino that had a sports book. That business model isn't sustainable long-term—and certainly not in a shrinking market like Reno.

A very good friend of mine, Jay, told me about a job opening in Australia. He suggested we approach it as a team, where he'd be the oddsmaker and I'd be the bookmaker.

It sounded intriguing. First of all, I'd always had a great desire to visit Australia, this great love from afar. In my dreams, I could even see moving there. It seemed like a great country with great people.

Secondly, I had tremendous respect for Jay. He was a terrific guy on a personal level and one of the most revered oddsmakers in our industry. Working with him would be enjoyable on multiple levels.

Mike, who wanted to hire us, had an Australian company that booked a lot of horse racing action in Oz and eastern Asia. His sports business consisted primarily of soccer action from the world's top leagues and international cricket. His

Australian customers also bet Australian Rules football, which hardly anyone else ever bet. He was getting almost nothing on American sports. This is where he wanted Jay and me to help him establish a footprint.

Oddsmaking versus Bookmaking

They may sound like the same thing, but they're not. A bookmaker has to be an oddsmaker to some degree, but an oddsmaker isn't always a bookmaker.

Once the odds are established, a lot of nuance goes into making book, which entails creating and presenting the lines to the public and managing the sports book's portfolio. Certainly, it's to a bookmaker's advantage to know really good oddsmakers who can lend their expertise. I was fortunate to know Roxy, along with others through the years, who made my job easier.

Mike flew us to Melbourne and put us up in the Crown Hotel and Casino. Jay and I each had our own suite and we agreed they were by far the nicest hotel rooms we'd ever stayed in. Every day Mike took us to his office, where we got a dose of how his business operated. Mike was a big believer in data and his team was constantly poring over reports and doing research on their computers. I have to say it was very impressive.

Mike knew how to live, too. He was a king in his world. The daily lunch deliveries were outstanding. Mike fed the office with fare from some of the area's best eateries, representing a number of ethnicities in Melbourne. For example, it has the second biggest Greek population in the world, behind only Athens, which certainly warmed the cockles of my heart. There are also Italians, Middle Easterners, Asians, Pacific Islanders … heck, just keep running the list to include every group from everywhere. And we had the best food from a bunch of them.

While Mike worked and ran his operation during the day, he took Jay and me out to dinner every night to discuss our plans for his venture into booking American sports. Mike took care of everything in Melbourne's most exquisite restaurants. It was a glutton's paradise.

One thing continuously surprised Jay and me, however. Mike never talked to us about the future of the business. He told us how he booked some high rollers and whether they were horse or sports bettors. He regaled us with how smart he was and how he got the better of so-and-so gambler. This went on night after night. We were scheduled to be in Australia for nine days and this went on for a solid seven days and nights.

I started to wonder if Mike and Jay had some sort of secret alliance of which I wasn't aware. But in fact, Jay had the same thoughts about me. We tried to steer the conversation to *our* business and the reason we'd made this 12,000-mile trip, but he talked right over us to go back to his favorite subject, himself.

Finally, two days before we were scheduled to go back to America, Mike called the two of us into his private office.

"Listen, mates," he said, "I've decided you two aren't the guys to lead my American operation. I've decided to take it in a different direction."

No one likes being fired, or not hired, or told you're the wrong direction, but by this time both Jay and I were relieved to not be working for this egomaniac. We figured we'd enjoy Melbourne for our last couple of days in a country we'd both grown to love, even in that short time.

Mike had other ideas. "I want you two to go to Darwin and take a look at my online operation there for a couple days," he said as he handed us a package of airline tickets.

The distance from Melbourne to Darwin is about the same as Miami to Minneapolis—a long freaking flight. And we had a stopover in Alice Springs, literally in the middle of the Outback by Ayers Rock, or Uluru as the natives call it, right where the dingoes ate Meryl Streep's baby in that movie. Oh, and our flight was scheduled for 5:30 a.m. Even though we'd been in Australia for a week, our body clocks had no fucking idea what time it was.

That wasn't all. The following day, we had to take another early-morning flight from Darwin to Sydney, then connect in Melbourne for our flight back to Los Angeles, then on to Las Vegas. The only way this could be worse was if he wanted to stick bamboo shoots under our fingernails to enhance the pain during these next two days of what was, ultimately, torture.

That night Jay and I went to dinner, alone, and talked about the situation. We both had the identical feelings of anger and disappointment at the rejection, but we were even more relieved than before at not being under Mike's thumb for the foreseeable future. Jay was single, so he was much more mobile than I was. However, if I moved to Australia, I'd certainly bring my kids with me, no easy task. And Mike having a lot of control over my life wasn't a very comforting thought, considering how volatile he was.

As the night and the conversation wore on, I knew there was no way I was going to Darwin in the morning. By that time, I convinced Jay to bail on that end of the trip as well.

As soon as we got back to the hotel, I mustered up my courage to call Mike. I had no doubt Mike was the kind of boss who didn't like his ideas being trumped by anyone. Nonetheless, I called him from my suite with Jay by my side.

"Mike, this is Chris. I've decided I'm not going to Darwin in the morning. You've made your decision to go another direction, which is fine, but there's nothing in it for me to take that flight to Darwin."

"Why, you son of a bitch! Who the fuck do you think you are?" he screamed at me. "You weren't even my first choice. I wanted ..." he mentioned another Las Vegas bookmaker, but no sense in dragging him into this. He was and still is one of my best friends. "You're nothing but the bloody third division!"

It was clear that Mike didn't have a ton of respect for my career in Reno. On the other hand, if he was going to hire anyone, including the likes of me, he might have done a little more homework.

"I'm so glad I didn't hire you."

"Well, Mike. You're certainly entitled to your feelings, but they just prove my point that there is no reason for me to go to Darwin to consult with you on your operation there."

"You cocksucker. I'll bury you so far in the Outback they'll never find you. You'll be dingo food."

"Well, Mike, you're just reinforcing my decision."

"Does Jay feel the same way?"

"Yes."

"Put him on the phone."

A couple things. First, I'm not much of a screamer, though I've been known to raise my voice on occasion, as I'm sure an ex-wife or employee would be more than happy to confirm. However, it takes a lot to get me into a shouting match. I didn't take the bait with Mike, and even though I was speaking quite sternly, it was at a lower decibel level than what would be considered shouting. Still, it didn't take a psychologist to tell this wasn't the most pleasant conversation, even only listening to my end of it.

Secondly, Jay is about the nicest person ever. When you first meet him, you think, can he really be this nice? Then you get to know him and you see that he is. He's so nice, he can be a little naïve at times, because he only sees the good in anyone until he's proven wrong. Even now, Jay was still mentally giving Mike the benefit of the doubt.

"He wants to talk to you," I said to Jay.

I immediately went to the closet to get my clothes. I grabbed my shirts and pants while they were still on their hangers and tossed them into my suitcase, just like they did in those old black-and-white movies. I had visions of Katherine Hepburn and Cary Grant as I packed.

In the most pleasant voice you ever heard, Jay said into the phone, "Hello, Mike. How are you?"

Even now, years later, if I say, "Hello, Mike. How are you?" to some of our friends, they start laughing. They can just see Jay in his naïveté not picking up on the tone of the conversation Mike and I were having. He didn't get it, even with me packing my suitcase like I was ready to flee like a fugitive. Which I was.

To his credit, it didn't take long for Jay to figure out exactly what was going through Mike's mind. He threatened Jay with the Outback funeral and his remains winding up in the belly of a dingo, just like he had with me. Jay began shouting at Mike, which I'd never heard before, then hung up and looked at me with as much fear in his eyes as I had in mine.

"Let's go," I said. "We've got to get out of here."

"Where are we going?"

"I have no fucking idea, but we're going. Now." By this time, I was completely packed. If there's some sort of record being kept, I'm sure I broke it.

We went to Jay's suite and he was packed and ready about as quick as I was.

We went to the lobby, dragging our suitcases behind us, and tossed our keys to the front desk. "We're checking out," I informed them.

They looked at us, knowing something was obviously wrong. It was close to midnight by then. "Would you like a receipt?" they asked in the midst of our fleeing.

"Nope," I called over my shoulder.

Fortunately, a line of cabs was waiting. We hopped into the first one and told the cabbie to just go. We still had no idea where.

My experience with cabbies in big cities is that they come in two types. You have the immigrants who just arrived or the veteran local who knows just about everything to know about what's going on in his town. Luckily, we stumbled into the second kind.

"Where to, mates?"

"Just drive for now."

I'm sure it was pretty obvious that we were on the lam from someone. After all, every crook and wiseguy in Melbourne hangs out at the Crown. And here we were, two Americans toting our luggage at midnight with no particular place to go.

We told the driver we needed to go somewhere inconspicuous, where we wouldn't be found. He took us to the absolute seediest place I have ever had the misfortune of laying my head to sleep. There is no more perfect example of the cliché "the penthouse to the outhouse" than when Jay and I went from the Crown to this dump. We also had to keep our fingers crossed that the cabbie wouldn't double back and try to figure who we were running from. The big tip we dished out probably helped, but you never know; it could also have been a tell about how desperate we were.

As we settled into the Melbourne Cockroach Arms, we realized we had another problem. We still had to get out of the country. We didn't want to take our scheduled flight, in case Mike had someone patrolling the airport looking for us.

Neither of us cared to experience that one-way trip to the Outback.

We decided that rather than try to get out of Australia early, we'd wait an extra couple days. By then, Mike might figure he missed his chance to find us and we somehow avoided him and got back to the States.

Mike had paid for the tickets and by rights, any changes had to go through him. Of course, that wouldn't work. Fortunately, the gods were smiling upon us for some reason and we found a Greek ticket agent. Thank God my people are notoriously clannish. Plus, very little will bring more joy to a Greek heart than screwing the Man. I started talking Greek to this young lady and

217

with a nod and wink—and a couple hundred-dollar bills—she was more than happy enough to change our reservation.

Jay and I made it back to America. I think we're probably safe now from Mike.

But every so often when we're having lunch with the boys or in a poker game, someone wants to hear the Australia story again. God knows they've all heard it plenty of times. No matter. When I get to the "Hello, Mike. How are you?" part, they all still laugh like the first time they heard it.

Chapter 19

"Nicky, We Might Get Him Today"

In October 2003, I left Cal Neva and went to the Golden Nugget. I had valid reasons for leaving, though with the benefit of hindsight, it was about the stupidest move of my life. A few good things came out of going to the Nugget, very few, but one of them was working with Nick Bogdanovich.

Nick grew up in Las Vegas, though his family wasn't in the casino business. He started writing tickets at the Sands sports book and worked his way up the ladder. He was an assistant sports book manager, then manager at Binion's Horseshoe. After that, he ran the sports book at Mandalay Bay. There, he had an issue that involved a well-known and very popular celebrity that resulted in Nick getting fired. Google the rest if you want the details, but I—and everyone else who knows Nick—thought he got fucked.

The typical suits that now run Las Vegas might not like Nick. He's not their kind of guy. He just doesn't fit the corporate image. Even my wife, when she first met him, said she wasn't so sure about him. But amongst our group, no one (except Zach) is more loved than Nick. I think my wife even has a little crush on him. And I will tell you that as for me, I absolutely love the guy.

However, I can see where people who don't know him would get the wrong idea. There are nice guys and good guys. Nick is not necessarily a nice guy, but he's definitely a good guy. Some people are both nice and good. Some people are neither nice nor good. But the worst are the nice guys who aren't good guys. They're the kind who'll deceive the hell out of you. They're "Polite Samaritans." If I were in need, I'd much rather come across the "Good Samaritan." The Polite Samaritan will say all the right things and act like he cares about you, but when it comes down to it, unless there's a way for him to benefit, he'll bail on you. Nick Bogdanovich is a guy who might not say the right thing, but there's no doubt he'll do the right thing. Two thousand years ago in the right place and time, he could have been the model for the Good Samaritan.

Anyway, enough kissing Nick's ass, except to say that he's one of the best and sharpest bookmakers anywhere.

When I got the job at the Golden Nugget, one of the first things I did was hire Nick as my second in charge. He'd been de facto blackballed since the escapade at Mandalay Bay, but I didn't give a shit. I needed him for some of the things I planned to do at the Golden Nugget. I wanted the best guys I could get on my team and Nick was definitely that.

One thing we did when we took over the sports book was put money lines on everything. If two teams were playing, we had a money line. Needless to say, some of the numbers were astronomically high. The mighty high straddles (the difference between the take and the lay prices) on some of those games left us a lot of leeway as bookmakers. A football game might be LSU vs. Louisiana-Monroe, where LSU would be -20000 (bet $20,000 to win $100) and ULM +7500 (bet $100 to win $7,500). A basketball game with Duke and Presbyterian might be about the same.

I've seen bookmakers over the years who wouldn't put up high money lines. How could an NFL game, any game, not have a money line? It's a pro football game, for God's sake. Any team has a chance to win. I asked them why not and the answer was always the same, "They're too high." Then I asked if they were afraid of the favorite or the dog and not a single one of them gave me a concrete answer. If you don't know who has the edge, that seems like a proposition that would be good to book.

Let me tell you, we put up those huge money lines and we took plenty of two-way business. It was great. Being the only book in town that isn't afraid to take a bet gives you a huge advantage and we capitalized on it.

One guy, Mel, loved to parlay the favorites. I might throw around words like "love" occasionally when they really don't fit, but in this case it did. He bet $100,000 on parlays with the two biggest chalks on the board. At times, his parlays barely won over $1,000. If he was really stepping out, they might win as much as $3,000, but those were pretty rare. Needless to say, he cashed a lot of tickets. A few of our co-workers, and even the higher-ups, tried to get us to quit taking his action. He was picking our pockets a few times a week at a couple thousand a pop.

But Nick and I stuck to our guns. The odds spoke for themselves and we knew it, even if the others couldn't see the big picture. Besides, we wrote mostly dog action on those kinds of games, so while Mel was winning, most of our customers were losing on those exact same games. It's called "bookmaking." What's more, if he ever lost even one of those parlays, he'd never get even.

Mel was quite a character. He was about 80 years old, another tough old Jewish guy from Brooklyn. A lot of them became successful in various walks of life, but almost to a man, they had it tough growing up. Virtually all of them were a first or second generation of poor immigrants who were horribly discriminated against in their home countries. Many of them became doctors, lawyers, or captains of industry, but none had it handed to them. They were tough as nails. Some gained a little couth and tact along their way and some didn't. Mel didn't.

I always got along with those crusty old bastards. I don't

know why. My wife and my ex-fiancé will tell you it's because I'm one of them. I'm not, really, but I do have more of that in my personality than I like to admit. A lot of guys around town didn't like Mel, but I did. I would kind of laugh or shrug off his old bastardly ways. Deep down, he was actually a pretty good guy.

Though Mel was only about 5'7", he was still in pretty good shape for someone his age. He used to box in the Marines and he got a big kick out of taking his stance and throwing jabs in my face, purposely just missing by inches. "Come on, tough guy," he said. "Think you could whip this old man's ass? Let's see it."

"Would you stop it? You're gonna hit me one of these days."

"You better hope I don't. I'll knock you on your ass."

I just laughed. A few years back, he probably would have.

One of the defining characteristics of those tough old Jewish guys is they've seen the worst—the worst of businesses (the Depression) and the worst of humanity (the Holocaust). So every night, Mel cashed out his tickets and took the money home. All the money. This multi-millionaire 80-year-old rode the bus to and from the Golden Nugget every day, with his money in a satchel, the kind of book bag students used to put their school books in before backpacks got popular. I tried to convince him to leave the $100,000 in a marker in the cage and just bet off that every day. That was what he bet all the time; I can't remember any variation. But he wouldn't hear of it.

"You guys might be broke in the morning," he said. "Besides, no one is tough enough to take it off me. I'd kick their ass."

"Mel," I responded, "you aren't tougher than a gun."

It didn't matter; he wanted his money every night. He was a kid when the Depression hit in '29 and I'm sure his early childhood reinforced what happened to the whole world, but to New York in particular during those days. In his mind, if some of those guys could go bust, so could the Golden Nugget.

As basketball season wore on, I noticed his payouts were

getting incrementally bigger. He was starting to get a little more gamble to him.

Occasionally, he played a side that was only -2000, which was really stepping out for him. By the time the NCAA tourney came around, he was probably up over $40,000 on us. And he was getting cocky.

In the first round of the tourney, Mel parlayed all the #1 and #2 seeds, winning them all. The one flaw in the seeding process is the second round is never easy for the top seeds. Number-one seeds play the #8/#9 winner and the #2 seeds play the #7/#10 winner. Those are never easy games. As a result, we can and do see some real upsets in the second round of March Madness.

Then one day... in 2004, Gonzaga was a #2 seed that advanced easily over Valparaiso in the opening round. The University of Nevada-Reno Wolfpack beat #7-seeded Michigan State in its opening-round game. The Nevada win was an upset, but they'd also beaten Kansas earlier in the year, so it wasn't a complete shock to anyone who followed college basketball. This was probably the most talented team in the history of Nevada basketball.

Mel showed up and even though Gonzaga was only -800 on the money line, Mel put them in his parlay. I remember taking the bet and just as Nick was walking by, I turned to him and said, "Nicky, we might get him today."

He looked at me and said, "Are you just saying that because it's Nevada?"

"No. I'm telling you, they have a big shot today."

Nick just nodded his head and went about his business.

To make it clear, I've been a UNR fan since moving to Reno. I'm not a nut over the team. I root for them, but they're not in my DNA like any of the teams I grew up with from western Pennsylvania. However, I'd watched this team quite a bit and knew they were very good.

Nevada dominated Gonzaga from the start, beating them

91-72. They were up 47-32 at the half. It was a real whupping.

One thing I've noticed over the years is that when someone bets nothing but the "sure winners" and finally loses, it completely upsets their equilibrium. They can't understand it. Their world is shaken, rattled, and rolled. Roxy always called it the "Tilt Factor." I can't think of a better phrase.

They definitely go on tilt. Mel was no different.

We now had him stuck for a little less than $60,000 and damned if he didn't want it back. His two-month run of kicking our asses would essentially have to be doubled to get even. College hoops was ending, so all he had in order to catch up was basketball and baseball. Have you ever watched the NBA? Have you ever watched the MLB? Sorry. The favorites, even the big favorites, lose all the time. That didn't stop Mel, though. He won a few parlays, then lost one. He started cutting back his bets, but he was still going for $30,000-$40,000 a rattle. I'm not sure how much we beat him out of before we stopped taking that kind of action, but it was a ton. I almost felt a little bad. Almost—I knew he was loaded, mostly through investing in Las Vegas real estate. He wasn't going to starve.

Bettors and bookmakers alike, take heed. If you're continuously betting a lot to win a little, it will eventually catch up with you. If you're booking this kind of action, as long as you have the bankroll to withstand a guy winning a whole lot before he finally loses, keep taking the action. Two-way play, which I was getting, makes it a lot easier to withstand, that's for sure. But if your numbers are right and your straddles are high and wide enough, you should be fine. It just might take awhile.

And always let the other guy go on tilt.

Epilogue

When I moved to the Golden Nugget in 2003, Bill McHugh had been replaced as CEO and the new boss didn't have a grasp on what we were as a company; he took us in new directions, accelerating the downward trajectory that had been going on for some years. Eventually, Jeff Siri, a good friend and very competent CEO, replaced him. However, the downturn had a life of its own. Our marketing plan was completely ineffective. We were in desperate need of some new capital, but the owners were in the habit of taking every available penny in the form of dividends. The only department that was successful was the sports book. I was paid quite well for running it, but I could also see the end of the line coming for that particular gravy train.

A bit before that, my cousin sold his online travel company, Travelscape, to Expedia. He and his business partner made about $100 million each and were shopping around for another deal, preferably having to do with casino gaming. While the Cal Neva was going through its troubles, a group of stockholders, primarily Warren Nelson and his family, were looking to cash in their shares. I approached my cousin to explore the possibility of his buying out the departing partners. He and his partner were definitely interested; they met with the Cal Neva principals and I thought the discussions went well.

Another piece to the puzzle was the Cal Neva held an

additional non-restricted gaming license. New non-restricted licenses in Washoe (Reno) and Clark (Las Vegas) counties are granted only to casinos that have hotels with a required minimum number of rooms. It wasn't always this way. Many casinos, like the Cal Neva, were built and operated before the restriction was implemented and those old licenses were grandfathered in.

Cal Neva had its own non-restricted license and it acquired another one when it purchased the Reno Turf Club. The Turf Club license was particularly valuable, because the building was condemned by the city as part of a major infrastructure project—digging a two-mile-long trench in order to lower the railroad tracks and separate them from a dozen street-level vehicle and pedestrian crossings throughout downtown Reno. The city and county granted the Cal Neva the right to move the license to another location anywhere within Washoe County, pending approval.

All in all, the deal was perfect for my cousin. And with his and his partner's millions, plus their track record of taking a company to the Promised Land, Cal Neva should have jumped at the chance to sell to them. Unfortunately, the principals valued the property way beyond what it was worth, which they'd done for years. They let my cousin's offer dangle until he lost interest and moved on. A big part of my frustration was how they botched that deal.

Not long afterward, my cousin and his business partner formed a group and acquired the Golden Nugget casinos in downtown Las Vegas and Laughlin. As they were putting together their management team, they offered me the position of race and sports book director.

Their plans for how they wanted to run the book were aggressive. I looked over the figures from the previous owner, MGM/Mirage, and saw a clientele that would be tough to beat. I meant that literally. At that time, downtown Las Vegas catered to some of Vegas' sharpest bettors, who made the rounds at the numerous books that were all within walking distance. The win percentage at downtown sports books was very low and the only reason the Golden Nugget sports book showed a profit on paper was because of how accounting distributed the company-wide allocation.

I explained to my cousin's group that the way they wanted to run the book was fine for the long term, but in the short run, it would be extremely difficult to turn a profit. They indicated that they understood my position and were seemingly on board with it.

Seemingly.

Though the offer they made me was on the high end of what sports book directors were earning at the time, it was quite a bit less than my overall package—salary, ownership points, and bonus structure—at the Cal Neva. On the other hand, I believed that taking the job with my cousin was the best long-term decision for my family, not just my wife and five kids, but also the whole extended family. With visions of a casino empire rivaling the biggest conglomerates in Las Vegas and the entire gaming world, plus assisting in the success of my family for generations to come, a cut in pay was a sacrifice I was willing to make.

The casino immediately started turning in some huge revenue increases, but the expenses matched them. Running the sports book in the bold manner management wanted, we began putting on some big players, but with very few rules as to how we'd book their action.

"This isn't especially advantageous to us as bookmakers," I explained to my cousin.

"Don't worry about it. These same guys are big players in the pit."

Even though I knew we were dealing from a position of weakness and it would be extremely difficult to make any money, I did what my cousin believed was in the best interests of the casino. Once the losing started, however, the story changed quickly. Now, pressure to win in the sports book came from everyone in the company. Problem was, when I tried to rein in the bigger players, they went over my head to my cousin, who overruled me. He even moved the lines on games and monkeyed with the rules without my knowledge. This is when I realized that you can't be the boss when you're not the boss.

It wasn't just my department; the whole casino was in the same boat—totally mismanaged and in turmoil. Things got so fucked up in the sports book, it was a monumental task just to straighten everything out. It took months to finally get the operation under control, jettisoning some customers who were taking advantage of us and coddling those we wanted to keep.

Then, just about the time I was beginning to feel we'd finally turned the corner, I was watching CNBC when the announcement came: The Golden Nugget was being sold to Landry's, the multi-brand (Rainforest Café, Bubba Gump Shrimp, Claimjumper, Morton's, the namesake seafood house, and 50 others) dining and entertainment company.

I was stunned. I had no idea this was coming.

I was left without a job.

As for my cousin, let me preface by saying that this was a kid I took into my home, no questions asked, when he was 16 years old and having trouble with his parents. I did the same when he was 21 and wanted to transfer to the University of Nevada-Reno to complete his college degree. My ex-wife wasn't in favor of either of those moves, but I made them anyway. I loved the kid and would do anything for him.

When he and his partners finalized the deal with Landry's, they made a huge score. You can look it up yourself if you're interested, but it was well over $100 million in profit for owning the Golden Nugget less than two years.

As for myself, well, let's just say that sports book directors' jobs aren't easy to come by. As of this writing, books are opening up in many new jurisdictions across the country following the big Supreme Court decision allowing states to legalize sports betting. Prior to this, however, full-service sports books were allowed only in Nevada and there were only so many directors' jobs to go around. I'd given up one of the best at Cal Neva. Admittedly, I was looking to move, but not for some 18-month gig. When I joined the Golden Nugget, I truly believed it would be the final job of my life.

Let me make this clear: From a purely business standpoint, my cousin did nothing wrong. I know how capitalism works. You put up your money and if the investment is successful, you make a profit. I didn't put up money. But I did invest my life and the lives of my family. I thought my cousin and his partners wanted to build a business, not just buy low and sell high. I never would have joined them if I knew that was their intent.

On my way out, my cousin loaned me a few months' salary. That was nice. However, I know that if I were starting a business and convinced a loved one or even a close friend to abandon a top job to join me and I subsequently made the score of a lifetime, that friend or loved one would share in my good fortune. Anyone who knows me won't doubt that it's the truth.

Had I remained at Cal Neva as a shareholder and race and sports book director, I would have been in a superb position to negotiate a lucrative buyout, perhaps along with a cushy job, when the partners finally sold the joint to William Hill, the race and sports betting giant. Instead, I was left scrambling for a decade. Don't get me wrong, things weren't exactly horrible. I made a living, but there were some difficult times, including my wife's health issues, some poor investment decisions, and IRS trouble. But I certainly could have had an easier time of it.

I've heard my cousin say that I'm one of his big disappointments in life. Well, the feeling is mutual. The Golden Nugget remains the only black mark on my bookmaking résumé over almost 40 years in the business.

My cousin's partner wrote a book about their experience

of owning and selling the Golden Nugget. I haven't read it, but I hear it's not bad. It would probably be of interest to anyone finishing up these pages. What bothers me is that he ends the book with four pages of thank you's. He names just about everyone he ever met in his life and anyone involved with the Golden Nugget. I treated this kid like a family member, too, because of his relationship with my cousin. I didn't get a mention. Neither he nor my cousin acknowledge what I personally sacrificed for them to achieve their dreams. Yeah. You're fucking welcome.

Obviously, there's some lingering bitterness over the whole Golden Nugget fiasco, but I moved on, recovered, and wound up doing well.

🖋 🖋 🖋

When I left the Cal Neva in 2003, I remained in their good graces. As William Hill was buying Cal Neva, my former partners there hired me to help them with the transition. And when William Hill was putting together what they called the "work streams" (accounting, human resources, legal, marketing, etc.), they named me head of the bookmaking work stream, which is the essential part of the business. I'm still proud of the work I did during that time and I received many compliments from everyone involved.

Then, when the final company team was being put together, William Hill made me a surprisingly insulting offer for employment and compensation. There was some political bullshit going on, of which I wound up on the wrong side, and I turned them down. I have some good friends at William Hill, including Nick Bogdanovich, the head bookmaker. But no love is lost between me and their upper management.

🖋 🖋 🖋

After leaving the Golden Nugget, I was hired by Vic Salerno and American Wagering. I was fortunate to land one of the few high-paying sports book jobs. Not only was the offer very attractive, but Jimmy Vaccaro had recently joined the company as well.

I was never an actual bookmaker for American Wagering; I was more of an ambassador than a day-to-day operations guy. I did a lot of radio and glad-handing. I made some good friends and had fun during my time there. In addition, the business increased during my tenure, so it was a success for all of us.

While I was working at American Wagering, a couple friends of mine, real Wall Street guys, were forming a hedge fund and wealth-management company. They asked me to be a partner and I accepted their offer. I put in a fair amount of my own money to get the project off the ground when we formed the company in October 2007.

Then, in November 2007, my wife, Pam, was diagnosed with a brain tumor.

Pam's story could easily be its own book, or at least a lengthy magazine feature. We went to Stanford for her surgery. She spent more than 18 hours on the table during that first operation and was on the critical list for a week. Many times, I thought we might lose her. She spent the next three months in the hospital. After her release, she was under constant care for many more months. The tumor wasn't cancerous, but as I came to find out, a multitude of other variables were involved and she went through numerous other surgeries. Eventually, she healed, but more than 10 years later, she still hasn't totally recovered. She never will. She's well enough to live a normal life, but we constantly deal with a number of issues. Still, I feel blessed to have her in my life. While I was there for her during her crisis, she was also there for me as I faced my own health crises in the past year.

Pam's brain tumor delayed the opening of our hedge fund

and wealth-management firm from December 2007 to May 2008. Maybe you can see where this is headed. The financial world fell apart in the summer of 2008, only six weeks after we opened our doors. Had we opened as planned, we'd have had a chance to capitalize on the last stages of the bull market that was still churning along. Instead, that delay of a few months put us right in the teeth of a worldwide panic with the collapse of the real estate and stock markets. Thus, while leaving the Cal Neva for the Golden Nugget was the worst move of my life, forming Sierra Nevada Wealth Management was the unluckiest.

Luckily, however, I was still under contract with American Wagering when I formed Sierra Nevada Wealth Management. I told the CEO, Vic Salerno, of my plans to leave the company once my contract expired. He was okay with that; I was still fulfilling my duties as the Vice President of Northern Nevada Operations while I was helping to put together Sierra Nevada.

Vic and I had been friends and competitors for years. American Wagering was the parent company of Leroy's, a satellite sports book provider. Both American Wagering and the Cal Neva sports book were eventually bought by William Hill, but for many years, those two companies, which boiled down to Vic and me, battled for dominance in that space. Even though we competed hard with each other, we remained good friends. Vic was at the baptism of all three of my children, we were often at dinner together, and we played in the same regular poker game.

Vic was really a life saver for me. Pam suffered from her tumor and the subsequent care that went with it just as the economy turned sour and it started to look like we might go through a repeat of the Great Depression of the 1930s. It never got quite that bad, but Nevada, which had boomed for years, suffered one of the biggest market downturns anywhere in the world. Of course, Vic and American Wagering were right in the middle of the worst of it. Everyone who worked there was forced to take pay cuts in order to keep the company afloat.

I'd already announced my departure from American Wagering, but Vic kept me on the payroll and, more important, on insurance. Pam's doctor and hospital bills rose well into the millions. I'm sure Vic faced pressure from people inside and outside the company to terminate me, but he never did. To this day, I talk to Vic about how easily he could have shit-canned me, but he shrugs it off, saying, "I just couldn't do it." Vic can be as tough a businessman as you can go up against. However, he's also one of the most kindhearted people you'll ever know. And in that regard, Pam's and my story is Exhibit A. I hate to think what would have happened to Pam and me without Vic Salerno. I'll never forget what he did for us. God bless him.

✎ ✎ ✎

Today, my life in Las Vegas has come just about full circle—maybe not the complete 360 degrees, but damn close.

The Stardust, where I spent my first year or so in the sports betting business, is no more, leveled for the unfulfilled promises of the real-estate boom in the 2000s. Its gargantuan lot on the Strip is now owned by the Genting Group, a huge casino corporation based in Malaysia. Genting's $4.5 billion megaresort moved along at a snail's pace for many years, but is now scheduled for completion in 2021. The legendary Stardust is nothing but a fading memory to Las Vegans who, like me, lived through its heyday.

Likewise, the Barbary Coast, scene of my second sports book job, is long gone, though the building still exists; it's now owned by Caesars Entertainment and is called the Cromwell, with the super-hip Drai's rooftop beach club and a trendy restaurant run by celebrity chef and TV personality Giadia De Laurentiis.

Nowadays, the former owner of the Barbary Coast, Michael Gaughan, owns and operates the South Point, which is where I work. As you know from reading this book, my casino bosses over the years have ranged from not so good to very good, but Michael has to be at the top of the good list. When he hired me this time around, he told me the sports book was mine. Period. "Run it the way you feel is right," he said. I'd heard that before, but it was never sincere. Not so with Michael. Of course, I keep in constant communication with him, speaking to him daily. But he doesn't interfere. God bless Michael Gaughan. He's one heck of a casino boss and a truly great guy.

When I started at the Barbary Coast in 1980, Jimmy Vaccaro was my boss. Now, I'm technically Jimmy's boss, but that's really a joke. No one is Jimmy's boss. Jimmy is Jimmy and no one dictates anything to him. Even Michael laughs about it. Jimmy has a heart of gold, but he marches to the beat of his own drum. I might be his boss on paper, but I don't do anything that I don't run by Jimmy first. We might not agree on everything, but his input is as imperative as it is invaluable. He has helped me in so many ways, it's impossible to calculate. He's my *consigliere*, and no one in this business could possibly have a better one to lean on. I'm truly blessed in my present position.

When I went to work at the South Point sports book in February 2016, one of the first things I heard was that Michael Gaughan had made a deal with members of the Musburger family, who were creating VSiN, the Vegas Stats and Information Network, a radio/television broadcast centered on sports betting. Brent Musburger, a nationally known sports broadcaster for more than 50 years, was the face of it. However, Brent's brother Todd and nephew Brian did the real work in putting together the project. We were instructed to keep the project a secret until it was ready to launch in March 2017. We actually did keep it under our hats for more than a year. I look back now and I can't believe we actually pulled it off.

From its inception, Jimmy Vaccaro, Vinny Magliulo, and I were brought in as outside contributors. This is what separates VSiN from competitors. The three of us were and are real bookmakers. In establishing VSiN, Vinny was actually much more than that. He was there from the beginning, helping to manifest the whole project from conception to reality.

Vinny is another part of my full circle. I first met him at the Barbary in 1980. Vinnie was a dealer in the pit at the time, but he spent all his break time hanging out in the sports book—and eating peanut butter and jelly sandwiches in the employee dining room. Vinny eventually moved out of the pit and into the sports book at Caesars Palace, where he remained until 2000 when he took a job with John Gaughan, Michael's oldest son, who formed Las Vegas Dissemination Company, providing horseracing information. I'll let Vinny or Brian Musburger write their own books to provide the details, but those two got together to present the idea of VSiN to Michael Gaughan. We're well into the project now and the future is bright for VSiN. I appear numerous times during the week, usually opening Brent's show with a quick synopsis of the betting action for the day.

I also continue to do Gill Alexander's show on Mondays during football season.

If you recall from the Prologue, Gill's show is responsible in many ways for this book; the Story Time segment of the "Guessing the Lines" podcast inspired me to pull all the stories into book form. When we were putting together the talent for VSiN, I went to the wall for one guy, Gill. Fortunately for all of us, Gill's talent was recognized and he has been one of the stable ingredients of the company.

Shortly before joining Gill in his podcast, I formed my own company, Against the Number. The original concept was to provide information to bettors, handicappers, and sports media. We met with some Vegas sports book operators and high-profile media companies, but we couldn't sell them on the concept. We were also selling picks in order to provide revenue to the company. After toying with various concepts, we realized that picks were what the public really wanted to buy.

In many ways, selling predictions on what team will win what game is a bit of a dirty business, but we put a lot of effort into doing things the right way. As a company, we had almost zero complaints about our service. I picked the football games and I was on the money more than 57% for the two years I did it. I hired someone else to do the basketball and he was even better. I'd evolved the business to the point where I was happy with it and was making a very good living. Plus, it's always nice to work for yourself. Shortly after completing my second full year, however, Michael Gaughan called me with an offer to run his sports book. Even though my business was finally up and running the way I wanted, Michael's offer was too good to pass up. Once Pam gave the okay, I sold Against the Number and went to work at the South Point with Michael.

My partners in Against the Number were Matt Clark, a computer programmer and very sharp handicapper, and Bill Thornton, a major stockholder in the Cal Neva and a big supporter of mine personally. Matt had the concept and platform design for SHARPS, the information aspect of Against the Number. I still use the platform he created for my own handicapping and I feel extremely fortunate to have run into Matt and formed the company with him.

✑ ✑ ✑

Less than a year ago as I write this, the Supreme Court handed down its long-awaited decision on the Professional and Amateur Sports Protection Act (PASPA), the federal law that essentially limited sports betting to one state—mine—for the last 25 years. By a six to three vote, they flung the door wide open to legalized sports betting around the country. Michael Gaughan appointed a team of us to expand the South Point sports book operation.

As I've tried to make clear throughout these pages, those

who don't know any better believe it's easy open a sports book and start raking in a shitload of money. Everyone thinks they're an expert when it comes to sports betting.

A lot of serious education—and I mean high-level post-graduate schooling and training—is now taking place among regulators, legislators, governors, and casino owners who've never been associated with a sports book. They all have to understand how different gambling on sports is than what they're used to: lotteries and slot machines. A few get it, but most don't. Explaining it is one part of our mission.

The other part is getting them to hire the South Point and Gaughan Gaming, which is owned by Michael's son John, to run their sports books.

Then come the leagues. Naturally, they all want a piece of the action. NFL Commissioner Roger Goodell wants Congress to take action. I don't blame Goodell. It's a lot easier to bribe, I mean lobby, 51 senators than it would be to deal with 50 separate states and their various regulators. If they get the federal government involved, though, things can get screwed up awfully fast. They're the ones, after all, who passed PASPA in the first place. Most of us in the business are hoping that the individual states maintain their jurisdiction. At least a few of them should be able to get it right. And a few are all we need. We already have a hell of an operation. We'd just like to add a few more properties to our portfolio.

Stay tuned. It might be the next book.

🖋 🖋 🖋

So here I am. I have a terrific job working for Michael Gaughan at the South Point. I have a great crew that keeps me young. I work daily with a legend in Jimmy Vaccaro. I'm on VSiN with Hall of Famer Brent Musburger and friends Vinnie Magliulo and Gill Alexander. I have a great group of friends and am still close with my cousins Zach Franzi and Art Manteris. My wife Pam is doing better every day.

I see Uncle Jack at least a few times a week and have lunch with him every Friday. He's 90 now and even though he has some issues, he's still going pretty damn strong.

Life is good. I hope I'll be sticking around for at least a few more years, but even if I go tomorrow, I've told my family to make sure that at my funeral, everyone knows I had one hell of a life. I am one lucky *lucky* guy.

About the Author

Chris Andrews began his "unofficial" career in sports betting when he was a kid in Pittsburgh. His uncle, Jack Franzi, is a legend among bookmakers and wiseguys. Chris launched his "official" career in the sports betting industry as a ticket writer in Las Vegas in 1979. He rose quickly through the ranks and became the director of the sports book at the Club Cal Neva in Reno at the age of 25. He's now the sports book director at the South Point in Las Vegas.

Want More on Sports Betting? We Have It!

Sharp Sports Betting
by Stanford Wong

Wong's classic book on sports betting explains the logic and math behind solid strategies for betting sides, totals, parlays, and props, and identifies what are now referred to as "Wong teasers." The emphasis is on football.

Gambling Wizards
by Richard Munchkin

Gambling Wizards takes you into the lives and minds of some of the most successful professional gamblers of all time, including famed sports bettors Billy Walters and Stan Tomchin, and horse-betting phenom Alan Wood.

Fantasy Sports, Real Money
by Bill Ordine

Compete in the daily fantasy sports game—football, baseball, basketball, hockey, even golf—using pro strategies and case studies from players who've won millions.

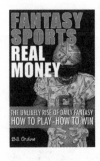

Weighing the Odds in Sports Betting
by King Yao

King Yao conveys the fundamental concepts necessary to succeed at sports betting, then applies those principles to strategies for betting sides, totals, halves, season wins, parlay cards, sports pools, and more, while also addressing advanced concepts such as hedging, middling, and correlation plays.

Gambling 102 by Michael "Wizard of Odds" Shackleford

The sports betting chapter of *Gambling 102* imparts basic strategies that are valuable for all levels of player, but are particularly beneficial for beginners. This book similarly provides basic strategies for all of the major casino games.

Other Games Too!

It's not only sports betting. At LasVegasAdvisor.com, you'll find the best books, software, and strategy cards for blackjack, poker, video poker, slots, and all gambling games.